They're *Lying* to You!

10 Lies That Shape Your Truth

JIM DEMINT

CONSERVATIVE
PARTNERSHIP
INSTITUTE

They're Lying to You:
Ten Lies That Shape Your Truth.

CONSERVATIVE PARTNERSHIP INSTITUTE

Dedicated to Truth

This book is brought to you by the Conservative Partnership Institute (CPI), an organization dedicated to preserving and promoting American greatness by supporting and building the Conservative Movement in America.

CPI was co-founded by former U.S. Senator Jim DeMint who continues to serve as Chairman of our Board. Our primary mission is to train, equip and unite Conservatives on Capitol Hill.

From the moment new Members of Congress arrive in Washington, place their hands on the Bible, and are sworn in, the Establishment has a well-oiled machine geared up to "teach" them how Washington really works. This is the Swamp. Those who aren't seduced by political favors are isolated by the Establishment and sometimes even targeted for defeat.

CPI was built to be the anti-Swamp. We embrace, support, and train Conservatives to successfully fight for freedom before they have been co-opted by the Left and Establishment.

The Left in America has created an alternate reality based entirely on Big Lies. This book exposes these lies with real facts. Please read this book and pass it along to friends who need to know the truth to help us save America. And, help us give more of these books away by visiting our website and supporting our work at http://secure.conservativepartnership.org.

Ed Corrigan
President, Conservative Partnership Institute

*To all who are willing to tell the truth
and to those who can handle it.*

Table of Contents

INTRODUCTION: HOW LIES CAN SHAPE YOUR WORLD

I am an old white guy in a dark suit with a MAGA hat. And if you just threw this book across the room, you've probably proved its point.

Without knowing anything about me, you profiled me. Your brain, conditioned by years of life experience and political indoctrination, filled in the rest of the story. I must be a privileged, racist, bigoted, white nationalist, homophobe, hateful, narrow–minded, gun–loving, Bible–thumping, rich, sexist, misogynist climate denier.

How am I doing?

Armed with this "knowledge," a lot of people will prejudge me. They won't trust me, and may even dislike me. They won't listen to anything I say, and feel righteous and justified in saying bad things about me—especially on social media, where countless followers can anonymously share scathing attacks and put–downs.

None of what I just described requires any argument, or even serious thought. This kind of snap judgment functions more like a Pavlovian reflex. It's impossible for us to wrap our head around the vastness of an uncertain world, so we pick up cues and clues to categorize all the things we don't fully understand. Our prism becomes mental shorthand.

Everyone does it. When conservatives see a college kid with pink hair and a Bernie Sanders button on his backpack, they'll jump to a lot of conclusions, too. Everyone has these personal prisms, regardless of our age, ethnicity, religion, politics, education, and experiences. And we don't just use them; we also *add to them* all the time.

The same process teaches us that working hard at school yields better grades, and praise from teachers. You notice that being nice helps you get what you want. You notice old people drive too slowly. You suspect people living in big houses are selfish, and that teenagers driving expensive cars are spoiled. Over time, these impressions harden into deep ruts in our minds: *all* old people are bad drivers, *all* rich kids are spoiled brats, etc.

These impressions explain why older people have granite paradigms that often block out new information altogether. They tend to be more set in their ways, trusting only "tried and true" solutions rather than "new-fangled fads." They base their prisms on their first-hand experience of what "really" works. These established belief structures can make older people close-minded and resistant to positive changes (it can also make them wiser). Their prisms can make it hard for them to see new ideas or judge them fairly.

I've experienced this myself. When watching a news channel reporting information I believe to be false, my prism blocks me from even considering whether the information might be true. I experience "brain strain," because the information sounds so inconsistent with *my* truth. I immediately deem the announcer misinformed or dishonest. Then I change the channel.

It's like the scene from *A Few Good Men*:

"I want the truth!"

"You can't handle the truth!"

For most of us, Jack Nicholson's famous line is right: we often can't handle the truth—if the truth doesn't fit into our worldview. We only accept "facts" that reaffirm what we already believe. But to stay sharp and thoughtful in an ever-changing world, we have to continuously evaluate our assumptions to be sure we're not being played for fools by people trying to manipulate us.

That's what this book is about.

In today's world, a saturation of personalized, electronic communications and commerce relentlessly competes for your attention—not just day by day, but second by second—click by click. All those advertisers, marketers, influencers, pundits, and content providers are really fighting over access to your mind, and how you make decisions. They either want to make you feel good by confirming something you already believe, spur you to action by provoking outrage about something you already dislike, or—most powerfully—manipulate your worldview by presenting something you dislike as something you must now love.

We're under this bombardment by manipulators all the time, so we all try to keep our guards up.

Very smart, well-paid people build careers manipulating the worldview of their fellow citizens; they sneak into our minds like wolves in sheep's clothing. Advertisers spend billions of dollars every year to convince people they won't be happy unless they buy this car, or attend that prestigious college, or get the latest and most powerful smartphone. Political advertising—both actual campaign ads and the more subtle activism practiced by so-called "mainstream" journalists and academics—is even worse.

Psychologists and advertisers have sophisticated explanations for all this manipulation. But in simple English, *they're lying to you.*

The most insidious lies in our society today share a common goal: pushing Americans to abandon their attachments to country, religion, traditions, and common sense.

I felt compelled to write this book because, over my life of nearly 70 years, in politics and out, I have seen firsthand how commitment to patriotism, faith, and hard work are essential to the well-being of our nation and every family in it.

I was raised in a relatively poor family with a single mom, but I saw how a good attitude and hard work could change my situation.

I have been married nearly fifty years, raised four children with my wife, and learned it's difficult to make a living and hold a family together. But working hard and nurturing a family is incredibly rewarding and helps build stronger communities.

In two decades running a business in South Carolina, I saw firsthand what living the American Dream can do to create jobs, opportunities, economic development, and interpersonal happiness in local communities.

I have also spent the past twenty years in the political fray in Washington, getting first-hand knowledge of the motives and strategies of both political parties. I've learned there are many people with different political views who have good intentions. I've also learned there are far too many purveyors of bad information for political gain. And I've seen an army of people creating paradigms built on outright lies.

Politicians know how paradigms work, and they are constantly trying to twist Americans' prisms to serve their interests. Presidential candidate Joe Biden once said, "We choose truth over facts." This may have been one of his many verbal bloopers, but it captures a phenomenon that is all too real in politics. There is a determined effort in America today to separate the Left's version of "the truth" from real facts.

I have written this book because America and future generations of our citizens depend on the wisdom and good choices of voters. We cannot make wise choices if our worldview is built on lies.

The political establishment—including both political parties, the media, academia, corporations, and entertainment industry— have used these lies for decades to shape Americans' personal filters.

And they have no shame in making up new lies to scare or shame you into allowing them to advance their radical agenda. Look no further than the Chinese coronavirus pandemic and the lies they tell to accumulate power and score political points. The virus is indeed a serious health risk for the elderly, but it became clear months ago that it poses much less risk for the majority of those under 50 and healthy. And the overwhelming scientific consensus worldwide is that children are at extremely low risk of sickness or death from the Chinese virus, and study after study shows they don't transmit the disease at the same rate as adults.

Yet governors, mayors, and bureaucrats nationwide and their media enablers all too gleefully flexed their authoritarian muscles to deny Americans basic rights this year in the name of "safety." If they believed their own lies, they would apply lockdowns equally —except they haven't done that at all. They've closed schools and churches, but call liquor stores and marijuana dispensaries essential services that must remain open. They arrest families attending Jewish funeral services in small groups, but praise and encourage thousands roaming streets in violent mobs burning cities and tearing down statues of American heroes including Abraham Lincoln and Ulysses S. Grant.

They have convinced so many people America is racist that

whenever political disagreements occur, "racism" has become the go–to slur. The same goes for "truths" like: climate change is an immediate and urgent threat; capitalism only helps the greedy rich; the federal government can solve all our problems; and Christianity is based on hate.

I hope this little book can begin to peel back some of the lies Americans are fed all the time. Each chapter will take up one of those lies, and in just a few pages punch some big holes in the wall of misinformation.

You might even start to wonder what else you have been told that just isn't so.

BIG LIE #1:
RELIGION IS HATE*
*Except the Religion of Progressivism

*"The first requisite of the happiness of the people
is the abolition of religion."*
— Karl Marx

*"They get bitter, they cling to guns or religion or antipathy
toward people who aren't like them or anti-immigrant sentiment
or anti-trade sentiment as a way to explain their frustrations."*
— Then–Sen. Barack Obama (D–IL)[1]

*"There's a gullible side to the American people. They can be easily
misled. Religion is the best device used to mislead them."*
— Michael Moore[2]

The Lie:

Belief in God and organized religion cause hatred and
oppress people.

The Facts:

• Religious Americans are less likely to commit crime, as violence
  decreases significantly in white and black communities as the
  percentage of residents who belong to congregations or attend
  services regularly rises. As one professor noted, "religious
  presence seems to matter to the amount of violence and crime
  in a community. It matters to blacks, whites, and Latinos."[3]

- Religious Americans are less likely to attempt suicide compared to those who report no religious affiliation.[4]

- Religious Americans are less likely to divorce, and more likely to forgive others.[5]

- Nearly two–thirds (62%) of religiously affiliated Americans make charitable donations, whether to religious or non–religious organizations, compared to less than half (46%) of Americans not affiliated with a congregation.[6]

- Religious Americans not only contribute to charity more often than the unaffiliated, they contribute more. One study found that religious individuals contribute more than twice as much as the unaffiliated, while a second found an even larger "giving gap"—$2,935 in charitable donations for church attendees, compared to $704 for those who do not regularly attend services.[7]

- Religious Americans give of their time as well as their treasure. The religious adopt babies and foster children at 2.5 times the national rate, provide most of the help to resettle refugees and mentor prisoners during and after their incarceration, and staff hundreds of thousands of alcohol recovery programs, unemployment assistance programs, and HIV/AIDS clinics.[8]

- A 2016 study found that religion and religious institutions contribute $1.2 trillion to the U.S. economy, more than the value of all but 14 of the world's economies.[9]

The Full Story

Don't panic, I won't try to evangelize you. But what you think about God determines how you think about everything. It is the single biggest driver of how you live your life. Think about it: if you believe there is a God who loves you and has a plan for your life and eternity, you will live very differently than if you believe you are an accident of evolution, with no hope of life after death.

What you believe about God is the most important factor in shaping your outlook on the world. And what your government believes about God will determine whether you can live in freedom.

That's why the first and biggest lie of the Left is that God either doesn't exist or is irrelevant, that morality is old-fashioned and discriminatory, and that organized religion is an oppressive scam handed down by generations of bigoted con artists.

The Left has a reputation for being godless, but that's not quite right. Lots of progressives go to church. However, faith on the left side of the political aisle has waned in recent years. Today, nearly 90% of conservatives identify as religious, while only about 60% of liberals do. That is a rapid change in the last 30 years, as only 12% of liberals identified as religiously unaffiliated in 1990.[10]

Yet even the liberals who don't regularly attend church services, especially the sort who run college campuses and media newsrooms, are not agnostic or atheistic.

They are downright devout. Social justice warriors and the "woke" are religious fanatics. It's just that their religion is politics, their church is government, and their high-priesthood is, well, themselves.

> Attorney General Bill Barr, in an interview with Mark Levin, said it better than anyone this summer:

> The left-wing has really withdrawn and pulled away from the umbrella of classical liberal values that have undergirded our society since our founding....[It] really represents [a] Rousseau-ian revolutionary party that believes in tearing down the system, that what's wrong about America today all has to do with the institutions we have, and we have to tear them down, and they're interested in complete

political victory....

> It's a secular religion. It's a substitute for religion. They view their political opponents as evil, because we stand in the way of their progressive utopia that they're trying to reach...For them this pilgrimage we're all on is a political pilgrimage. Everything is reduced to politics. For people who don't have that perspective, politics is important but it's not the whole purpose of life.[11]

Barr's reference to Jean–Jacques Rousseau can help conservatives understand how progressives came to worship the government. Rousseau, an 18th century philosopher that disagreed with American concepts of individual rights, argued that true happiness and freedom in life came only through submission to the government's will. And what happens if someone refuses to worship at the altar of government control and join the groupthink mentality of the political establishment? Rousseau's answer: "True freedom consists in the willing subordination of the individual to the whole of the State. If this is not forthcoming, compulsion is necessary; but this merely means that the individual 'will be forced to be free.'"

Sound familiar? Today's political Left, whether you call them liberals or progressives or Marxists or socialists, are radical authoritarians who worship the power of government. If you disagree with their definition of political correctness, they will force you to comply—whether by public shaming, charges of racism or sexism, or using the force of government to compel you to submit.

Secular elites and their institutions—from the academy to the media to the makers of popular culture—would have you believe their religion is actually science and reason. But that's a lie, too. The progressive paradigm relies heavily upon leaps of faith, many of which are indistinguishable from self–made idols and superstitions.

Now, I won't take the time to prove to you that God exists (though He does), or that the Bible contains important truths about our relationship with God and each other (though it does). I want to show that the incessant secular, progressive talking points about religion, Christianity, and science—and most especially, about secular progressives themselves—are self-serving propaganda. Their goal is not to liberate Americans from the strictures of religion, but to force *their* religion—progressivism— on everyone. Putting themselves in the place of God has been the goal of every tyrant who ever ruled.

Whatever name this ancient religious ideology goes by today— "atheism" or "secularism" or "scientism" or "liberalism," or silliest of all, "reason"—it's not just a big lie. It's a swindle—the theft of your foundation for logic and integrity.

Our beliefs about God, morality, and objective "Truth"—with a capital-T—are the most important factors in the development of our character. God provides a fixed foundation for right and wrong; without Him, morality becomes a matter of personal opinions and prevailing fads.

Religion, especially the Judeo–Christian biblical view, has given America the values and traditions that have made it unique in all the world. What makes religion so important to political debates is that it is upstream of politics—it shapes the way we think politically. Your political views on taxes or immigration probably don't impact your theological beliefs about Moses or Jesus or the Bible. On the other hand, your beliefs about Moses and Jesus and the Bible *very much* influence your views not only of taxes and immigration, but *every* political issue under the sun: foreign policy, abortion, criminal justice, education, etc.

One of the first principles of the secularist lie is the progressive "reading" of the First Amendment. They would have you believe the Framers did not guarantee "freedom *of* religion," they guaranteed "freedom *from* religion." According to this version of the Constitution, politics and policy are supposed to be "God–free zones"—forums for fact–based problem solving, not discussions of morality.

How many public debates about pornography, LGBT–related controversies, religious symbols in public memorials, or sex–ed curricula in public schools have been shut–down the moment a traditional religious believer makes an argument about biblical morality? Immediately, someone espousing the progressive prism will fire back, "You can't make religious arguments about policy. That violates the separation of church and state!"

It happens all the time. Often, many traditional religious Americans stay out of public debates altogether, to avoid retribution from the corporate, political, and cultural elites that dominate the Left. It is an extremely effective line of argument... except that it's a lie.

The Left has *no problem* making moral—even explicitly biblical and Christian—arguments in favor of policies they like. They do it all the time.

No progressive begrudges the Christian pastors whose sermons lit the fires of the abolitionist and Civil Rights movements. There isn't an elected Democrat in America who would deny that slavery was our Republic's "original sin." Part of the reason Martin Luther King, Jr. was such a persuasive and effective leader was that he was *the Reverend* Martin Luther King, Jr. King's religious training gave him the theological knowledge and nonviolent techniques to make a powerful moral case against the immoral system of racial segregation.

Rev. Jesse Jackson finished second in the Democratic presidential primary campaign in 1988. Back in the 1970s, Catholic priest Fr. Robert Drinan served ten years in the U.S. House of Representatives. In both cases, these men of the cloth were down–the–line leftist activists, so there was no choreographed media outrage about church and state.

Liberals advocate for welfare because we are "our brother's keeper" and because Christ called on us to "feed the hungry."
Open borders activists constantly shame immigration laws for denying families "room at the inn."

The Left's tirades against Wall Street always amount to a biblical sermon about the evils of greed.

Their resistance to tougher law enforcement during the long American crime wave from the 1970s to the 1990s always appealed to the Christian virtue of mercy.

And no leftist will ever second–guess citing the Bible or an appeal to a religious authority like the Pope, so long as it's in the service of stricter environmental or labor regulations that empower its own special interests.

Indeed, on "Earth Day" 2020, Pope Francis issued a proclamation that climate change shows mankind "has sinned against the Earth."[12] Of course there was no leftist outrage on Twitter or MSNBC, or press releases from Joe Biden's presidential campaign. They regard religious arguments in favor of progressive causes as perfectly fine.

So do I! And so should you.

There is nothing wrong with progressives making explicitly moral or religious arguments in favor of their preferred policies, just as there is nothing wrong with conservatives and Americans with more traditional beliefs doing the same thing.

The Left's "commitment" to "separation of church and state" is pure fiction. They have no problem with religion as such. What they hate and condemn are *other* religions, theological competitors to *their* religion of progressive politics.

When religious conservatives speak up, the Left usually doesn't grapple with the substance of their arguments. Rather, progressive politicians will try to disqualify opposition altogether by accusing moral traditionalists of trying "to impose your religious values on us."

But that is a lie. Look across the spectrum of political issues and debates. Religious traditionalists are almost always playing *defense*. There are no bills in Congress to force all Americans to live according to evangelical or Catholic or Orthodox Jewish moral teachings. The Left's constant harangues about "theocracy" are baseless. Indeed, they get things 180 degrees backwards.

That's because Americans value tolerance, respect, and freedom. Religious freedom—as defined in the First Amendment or advocated by religious Americans—is not about imposing anything on anyone. It is about giving every American, regardless of their faith, the freedom to live out their beliefs. Protestants, Catholics, Jews, Muslims, atheists, and everyone in between are equally free to practice their faith in public and private according to creed and conscience.

It is the *progressives* who seek to use the power of the government to impose their values on the rest of the country, to stamp out dissenters from the Left's religion of "woke-ism." The progressive prism is by definition absolutist, intolerant, and even theocratic. They approach religious "freedom" the way medieval monarchies did: people are only *free* if they believe what the government tells them to believe; dissent must be marginalized or eradicated. That's why major media outlets now routinely put traditionalists' concerns about *"religious liberty"* in scare quotes—to subtly inform readers that it's a made–up problem they shouldn't take seriously.

We don't even have to scour history to explore the Left's deep hatred of organized religion in general and biblical Christianity in particular. We can prove this point just looking back over the *past year.*

Last fall, at a town hall during the Democratic presidential primaries, one of the elite media's favorite candidates, former congressman Beto O'Rourke from Texas, called for the elimination of tax–exempt status for churches who would not marry gay couples.[13] O'Rourke, and the cheering crowd at the LGBT–issues forum, wanted to exempt from federal taxation only those churches who submit to the progressive prism on gay marriage.

During the national COVID–19 shut–downs in the spring of 2020, progressive mayors and governors singled out churches for criticism, warnings, and petty tyrannies. First, they ordered public religious services cancelled when other, far less fundamental enterprises like liquor stores and marijuana dispensaries could stay open. Then, when leaders of faith communities adapted and tried to serve their congregations while obeying social distancing guidelines, many government leaders banned perfectly safe observances like outdoor confessions and drive–in services. Kentucky's Democrat Governor Andy Beshear infamously ordered the state police to write down the license plates of any car parked in a church parking lot on Easter Sunday, so that the car owners could face proper punishment.[14]

No politician would order such police harassment on the parking lots of businesses or institutions that reliably embrace the progressive paradigm, like news media offices or abortion clinics.

During the COVID panic a Harvard Law School professor,

Elizabeth Bartholet, published a long scholarly article calling for governments to ban homeschooling.[15] Why? Because it's mostly a conservative Christian phenomenon. In an interview regarding her article, Bartholet explained her position: "[I]t's also important that children grow up exposed to community values, social values, democratic values, ideas about nondiscrimination and tolerance of other people's viewpoints."[16] By those buzzwords, she means "progressivism." And again, Professor Bartholet has *no problem* with teachers indoctrinating children with values. She just demands that they be *her* values. To the Left, "education" means five-day-a-week progressive Sunday school.

When pressed on their obvious double standard—indifference to progressive-leaning religious institutions, and open hostility toward traditional religious values—the Left rolls out its next lie: "traditional religious values are hate!"

This is really a "break glass in case of emergency" lie that lazy progressives resort to when they run out of ammo: like in old war movies where a desperate soldier fires his last bullet and futilely throws his gun at the enemy.

By progressives' own standards, it's nonsense.

In 2008, the Left practically deified then-Sen. Barack Obama (D-IL). Oprah Winfrey famously endorsed the Democratic presidential candidate because it wasn't enough just to tell the truth, "We need politicians who know how to be the truth."[17] Well, in 2008, Senator Truth ran for president while publicly *opposing* gay marriage. Is that because he "hated" gay people? Exit polls showed Obama beat Sen. John McCain (R-AZ) among LGBT voters by a more than two-to-one margin; did they somehow miss Obama's bigotry?[18] Of course not.

Nor does "hatred" impel some religiously observant businesses to conform to their religious values. It isn't hatred of hungry people that leads Chick–fil–A to close its restaurants on Sundays. It isn't hatred for distilleries and brewers that leads Latter Day Saints and Muslims to forego alcohol. It isn't hatred of LGBT people that leads some bakers and florists and ministers not to cater and administer gay weddings. It's not about hate; it's about loving something more than politics—which, to a progressive, is heresy all by itself.

Religious devotion makes pretty much every religious American a better version of himself or herself. It makes us more faithful, kinder, more honest, more respectful of differences and loving toward strangers. It makes us less judgmental. Christianity's standard is to "love the sinner and hate the sin" as the Bible states: "for all have sinned and fall short of the glory of God" and "in humility, value others above yourself."[19]

Compare that sentiment to social justice warriors' organized outrage toward all non–progressives. At *The New York Times*, columnist Bari Weiss recently resigned because she could no longer tolerate what has become "the 'new McCarthyism' that has taken root at [the nation's] paper of record."[20] Weiss said her colleagues attacked her "forays into Wrongthink" by calling her "a Nazi and a racist."[21] Whereas Christianity emphasizes love, humility, and meekness, progressivism emphasizes intolerance and contempt.

Religious faith empowers its adherents to rise above the weakness of human temptation, to aspire to the better angels of our nature. That is why, though it is thousands of years old, biblical religion is always fresh and new and revolutionary—it always and everywhere challenges entrenched power. It doesn't make believers perfect or even better than other people; it makes us better and stronger than we would otherwise be. If you know Christians who are nonetheless sinners—and, by the way, *that's all of us*—rest assured we would be much worse without a faith that calls us to love God and love others as ourselves.

History confirms the good that comes from religion—and the evil that comes from its suppression. It wasn't churches or synagogues but explicitly anti–religious, progressive *governments* —consumed with the contempt for dissent embedded in the progressive worldview – which launched the Reign of Terror in France, the Great Terror in Russia, the Holocaust in Nazi Germany, the Killing Fields in Cambodia, and the Great Leap Forward in China.

On the other hand, organized religion in general, and Christianity in particular, helped inspire the end of slavery around the world, the recognition of universal human rights, the foundations of civilized society such as private property rights and judicial systems, the scientific method, almost all the treasures of western civilization, and the successful movements to reform that civilization from within.

The founding of America was based in deeply religious roots, recognizing that basic human rights are not granted by a king or legislature, but "endowed by our Creator." Or as George Mason, the driving force behind the Bill of Rights, said even more clearly, "The laws of nature are the laws of God, whose authority can be superseded by no power on Earth."

Meanwhile, religious institutions make their communities *better off* for it. Religious Americans donate more than double to charitable organizations than the nonreligious. They volunteer their time to help the poor more often, they commit crime less often, and they start hospitals and schools to improve their communities.

The marriage of one man and one woman has been the indispensable building block of every successful society in human history. It motivates men and women to become better people, and creates the ideal environment to raise children.

Why They Lie

What the Left truly despises is not religion, but competition. The Left hates traditional religions as an alternative source of authority, with deep claims on individuals' loyalty and obedience. They hate that religion exists as an alternative infrastructure for morality and social reform, outside the halls of power that elites already control. And they hate that religion is so reasonable, so demonstrably good as attested to by both scientific inquiry and the historical record.

They hate that, despite all their efforts, the Bible is the best–selling book in the world, every single year.[22]

They hate that the Bible provides not only moral instruction outside the authority of government (and the progressives who control government), but that biblical morality works in ways government programs never can.

It is supremely ironic that many who reject religion have their own set of unquestionable, deeply unscientific dogmas: Unborn babies are "clumps of cells" or "potential life," in direct opposition to the unchallenged conclusions of embryology. A man can have a uterus and give birth to babies, in direct defiance to biology. Pre–pubescent children should be surgically mutilated, without their parents' consent, if the child would like to change their gender.

These beliefs are not products of hypothesis, experiment, and observation. They're just unquestionable myths, like ancient Greeks attributing lightning to Zeus or floods to Poseidon.

So, why all the lies about religion? Ultimately it's about power. For all its cultural influence, the Left is fundamentally insecure. Put more bluntly: their narrative is false, and they know it's false. So they use their cultural power, in the form of social media outrage mobs, corporate pressure, and political protests, to intimidate dissenters—the dangerous heretics!

Progressivism and Socialism depend on an all–powerful government. Religion—especially biblical Christianity—threatens government power.

Progressives know that organized religion is a source of morality and happiness and social solidarity outside their control. What's more, they know religion works, in ways their supposedly "secular" worldview doesn't, that it answers human needs and fosters human progress better than campus–and–newsroom "woke" bullying.

Faith in God and the Bible—because it's True—gives Americans a source of strength. And the progressive paradigm, because it is false, gives Americans a source of weakness and despair. Progressives tell their lies about religion because they know faithful people will be stronger people, and therefore a greater threat to their tenuous worldly power.

BIG LIE #2:
AMERICA IS RACIST AND EVIL

"Considering the history of this country,
how can you not be racist?"
— Don Lemon[23]

"Our country was founded on racism
—and is still racist today."
— Rep. Beto O'Rourke (D–TX)[24]

The Lie:

America was built on slavery, and is plagued with systemic racism today.

The Facts:

- Though he held slaves himself, Thomas Jefferson's original draft of the Declaration of Independence explicitly condemned the Atlantic slave trade, stating that King George III had "waged cruel war against human nature itself, violating its most sacred rights of life and liberty in the persons of a distant people who never offended him, captivating and carrying them into slavery in another hemisphere or to incur miserable death in their transportation thither."[25]

- Far from codifying slavery, the Framers hoped the Constitution would set America on a path to its abolition. As President in 1806, Thomas Jefferson proposed, and Congress subsequently enacted, an abolition of the slave trade. That law passed three weeks prior to Great Britain's abolition of the slave trade, and took effect on the first day possible under the Constitution.[26]

- In an 1852 speech, abolitionist Frederick Douglass endorsed the view of the Constitution as an anti–slavery document: "Take the Constitution according to its plain reading, and I defy the presentation of a single pro–slavery clause in it. On the other hand it will be found to contain principles and purposes, entirely hostile to the existence of slavery."[27]

- A 2013 study found Americans among the nationalities most likely to embrace a racially diverse neighbor, suggesting a greater degree of racial tolerance than most European, Asian, and African nations.[28]

- A 2018 Pew Research Center survey found that more than three times as many Americans support (61%) increasing diversity in their country than oppose it (17%). By contrast, much smaller percentages of citizens in European countries like France (49%), the Netherlands (41%), Poland (28%), Italy (26%), or Greece (17%) support increased diversity.[29]

- America has over 50 million foreign–born residents—the largest number of foreign–born residents in the world—and welcomes more than half a million immigrants as citizens each year. Over the last decade, the United States has naturalized more than 7.2 million citizens.[30]

- Racist views have greatly diminished in America over the last several decades. Indeed, polling questions on issues like school desegregation and interracial marriage "are no longer included on major national surveys; they have become essentially universally accepted by whites and therefore not deemed as worth asking on surveys."[31]

- Violent crime is the greatest predictor of police shootings, not race. Increasing the percentage of white officers involved in a fatal shooting did not increase the likelihood that the victim was of a racial minority.[32]

The Full Story

An essential part of the leftist worldview is to look down on America as part of a uniquely evil scourge upon the world.

This is the second most important lie the Left needs you to believe. First, they need to break the supernatural bonds between you and God; next, they need to break the natural bonds between you and your country. Patriotism—the special love of one's own nation and home—is part of human nature. It can't be erased. The lump in your throat you get when you read the preamble to the Declaration of Independence, the chill up your spine when you see Americans winning gold medals at the Olympics, the tear that comes to your eye when you hear Martin Luther King's "I Have a Dream" speech—these things may hold universal appeal, but they are uniquely special to Americans because they are part of *our* story. And what a story!

The history of the United States reads like a storybook full of real-life miracles. It's the story of poor, outcast dreamers who asserted and then fought for their rights against the most powerful empire the world had ever known, and won. Those dreamers led the world in embracing economic truths that over time pulled billions of the planet's inhabitants out of poverty. They twice rescued the old world from violent tyrannies. They led a revolution in education, medicine, and scientific discovery —all the way to the moon – and all while managing unique challenges as the most ethnically, religiously, and culturally diverse nation in the world.

How could anyone *not* love this place?

That's why so many foreigners apply for American visas and citizenship every year. America's progressive elites may not love America, but our immigrants—most of them poor, unprivileged, young men and women of color—do. Our immigration system is not overflowing with new applicants because America is an unjust, corrupt country that only works for people like me. It's because America can work for *everyone*, no matter who they are or where they come from.

As conservative commentator Ben Shapiro succinctly put it: "Freedom is what makes America unique, not slavery... Here is the truth about America today: America is not only the least racist it has ever been, according to statistics, it is one of the least racist multi-racial countries on the planet."[33]

But if America already *works*, then who needs all these progressives promising to radically change it?

That's the *real* story behind the Left's anti-Americanism Patriotism and America's real history are obstacles to progressives' plans because the more Americans love their country, the less they want to change the things that have made it great.

So the progressive Left has embarked on a multi-generational project of slashing away at that love, manipulating Americans' paradigm to convince them their country is deeply flawed and not lovable.

And in America today, the least lovable thing anyone can be is racist. "Racist" is the nuclear bomb of American political rhetoric —and rightly so.

Slavery was our nation's "original sin," and the evil of racism —racial supremacy, racial oppression, and racial violence— underpinned it. Slavery had been a fact of life across most human civilizations in history up to that point.[34] What makes America's experience different is that we were among the first countries to end it.

America's true story lies in an ongoing struggle to expand freedom for people of every race, religion, and gender. America has not only been a pioneer in ending oppression here at home, but has sent our own sons and daughters overseas to fight and die to secure the freedom of others.

In 1776, the American people asserted *universal* human rights to life, liberty, and the pursuit of happiness. We created a new nation, upon revolutionary principles of human dignity. But slavery clearly violated those principles. In his Second Inaugural Address, Abraham Lincoln blamed the hundreds of thousands of casualties in the Civil War as America's penance for our sin— drops of blood drawn with the lash being repaid by those drawn with the sword. And there is much truth to that.

Even after the Civil War, our redemption remained incomplete, to say the least. For another century, Jim Crow laws that legally mandated segregation, along with extra–legal oppression and violence, perpetuated racial segregation and discrimination.

Even with the litany of triumphs in America's history, the work to fully eradicate racism is ongoing, as the legacy of slavery and racism remains with us. To most Americans, this legacy increases our resolve to help our society move a little closer every day to the colorblind society our principles demand and Martin Luther King, Jr. once dreamed of.

To woke progressives, however, America's history of racial sins provides an opportunity to cynically impose their false narratives on the entire country.

Because of those sins, "racist" is about the worst thing someone in *America* can be accused of. It's also the worst thing America can be accused of.

If you are a political progressive seeking to change our country, you can lecture people about inefficient taxes or the budget deficit or Obamacare's failures until you're blue in the face. Most people's eyes will glaze over. But if you can attack someone or some policy for being *racist*, everyone sits up and takes notice, because everyone can understand that serious charge.

And so, one of progressives' big lies calls America itself irredeemably racist. When leftists refuse to stand for our nation's song or pledge to our flag, they are essentially denying their identity as Americans. Their protests oppose our country and what it stands for.

Why? Because to achieve their goals, they need you to believe that America is racist and evil.

The progressive paradigm does not say racism exists in America. It does not say racial discrimination still exists in America. It is not saying America has problems. It is saying America is the problem.

The most comprehensive and aggressive product of the progressive paradigm in recent years comes via the "1619 Project." This campaign, created by the *New York Times*, attempts to convince Americans of a new "truth," that everything they know about July 4, 1776 and the Declaration of Independence are lies. They intend to implant a new "truth" in every American's mind: The United States was *really* founded in 1619, when the first African slaves arrived in the colonies.

"Though America did not even exist yet," the *Times* wrote, "their arrival marked its foundation, the beginning of the system of slavery on which the country was founded."[35]

The first essay in the 1619 Project begins with an eye-grabbing assertion: "Our democracy's ideals were false when they were written."[36] It sounds bold and even revolutionary. But it's all nonsense.

First of all, "ideals" can't really be false. Liberty? Justice? The rule of law? Happiness? These things were not false in 1776, or in

1619, and they are not today. They may be more prevalent in some times and places than others. But you could say the same thing about bread or dinosaurs or pine trees. That doesn't make them false. So the *New York Times'* whole project starts with a *non sequitur.*

The *Times* probably didn't mean that America's founding ideals —freedom, opportunity, equality—were false, but that America's founding generation didn't live up to those ideals. Which of course is true, especially regarding the slave trade. But it is precisely America's commitment to those ideals—even when we fall short, as all humans do—that has made American history such an inspiring story.

The pursuit of racial equality is part of that history, and it began *during* that founding generation itself. Yes, Thomas Jefferson owned slaves. Does that make the words of the Declaration of Independence—"we hold these truths to be self-evident, that all men are created equal"—false? Of course not. As the essayist Andrew Sullivan wrote in *New York* magazine, those words "were, in fact, the most revolutionary leap forward for human freedom in history."[37]

The 1619 Project further asserts that "out of slavery—and the anti-black racism it required—grew nearly everything that has truly made America exceptional: its economic might, its industrial power, its electoral system."[38] Except that, again, slavery was practiced all around the world at the time. If slavery made America rich and powerful, why didn't it do the same for the rest of the world?

The *Times* goes on: "Conveniently left out of our founding mythology is the fact that one of the primary reasons the colonists decided to declare their independence from Britain was because they wanted to protect the institution of slavery."[39]

This is a lie! It is provably false. Only after seven months, and numerous protests from historians, did the *Times* finally amend the original article to say that "some of" the colonists – meaning a number as small as a handful – want to declare independence to protect slavery.[40]

The American Revolution had nothing to do with protecting slavery. The British were in the slavery business, and as such would not want to lose a market for their goods, including slaves. Americans fought the revolution to gain our independence from Britain. The Declaration of Independence details all the reasons Americans were willing to give their lives, their fortunes, and their sacred honor for freedom.

Remember, the very first American to die in the Revolution was an African American: Crispus Attucks, killed by British soldiers at the Boston Massacre. Not surprisingly, Attucks' story is conveniently left out of the 1619 Project's mythology.

The entire thrust of the 1619 Project is that America was, is, and always has been first and foremost an instrument of racial supremacy and oppression. That's not history; that's vandalism masquerading as history. And again, don't take my word for it. Soon after the Project launched, five of the most prominent historians in the world—Victoria Bynum, James McPherson, James Oakes, Sean Wilentz, and Gordon Wood,—trashed the project's sloppy, ideologically driven mistakes. Of the *Times*' assertion that the Revolution was fought to protect American slavery, they wrote: "If supportable, the allegation would be astounding—yet every statement offered by the project to validate it is false."[41]

Other mistakes were just as big and just as central to the 1619 Project's lie.

The *Times* said that Abraham Lincoln—yes, *Abraham Lincoln!*—was part of the great American conspiracy against black people.[42]

That is an obvious lie!

Two years before the Civil War, Lincoln ran as the anti–slavery candidate in a Senate contest against Stephen Douglas that featured the famous Lincoln–Douglas debates. In the Gettysburg Address and elsewhere, he spoke of how the Declaration's assertion of universal equality applied to all people, regardless of race. He publicly opposed slavery's expansion. He was elected president as an anti–slavery candidate of an anti–slavery party. Indeed, it was *his election* that spurred southern states to secede. Lincoln freed all the slaves he had legal authority to free—in Washington, D.C. and Confederate territory still in rebellion against the United States. And he shepherded the 13th Amendment, which finally ended slavery in the United States, through Congress. He famously wrote, "If slavery is not wrong, nothing is wrong."

But to the *New York Times*, none of this matters.

The 1619 Project says that in the long fight for civil rights, black Americans largely "fought back alone."[43] This is a cynical, dangerous, ahistorical smear. Black Americans obviously *suffered* under Jim Crow laws in ways even the most pro–civil rights whites never did. But the success of the civil rights movement arrived when Americans of all races came together, first in the court of public opinion, and later in Congress.

Martin Luther King's dream of a future where his children would be judged by the content of their character and not the color of their skin was *America's* dream, too. That's why the Civil Rights Act passed—as with the 13th Amendment, with the support of an overwhelming majority of *Republican* members of Congress.

The 1619 Project is the kind of historical revisionism that is clearly farcical to Americans who know their history—to anyone interested in the truth.

Thankfully, a group of black historians have come forward to refute the "truth" of the 1619 Project. They have countered with the real truth: the 1776 Initiative.

The 1776 Initiative is a "consortium of top black academics, columnists, social service providers, business leaders and clergy from across America who are committed to telling the complete history of America and black Americans from 1776 to present."[44] The real truth about racism in America is that the overwhelming majority of Americans of all races *are* not racist. And the handful of Americans who are racist are pathetic losers with deep holes in their souls that they try to salve with hate. But the Left uses these misfits, whom the rest of us denounce, to define the whole country.

In Minneapolis in early 2020, a black man was killed in the custody of police officers. For more than eight minutes, a white officer pressed his knee onto George Floyd's neck. He shouted, "I can't breathe!" He suffocated to death. And it was all captured on video.

This was terrible and tragic. We don't know whether the officer killed Mr. Floyd intentionally or was just overzealous and reckless. It doesn't matter. It was clearly unjust, unnecessary, and the officers involved should be held accountable.

But was this really a racial incident? In the wake of Floyd's death, that question didn't seem to matter.

The Left and practically all American media immediately announced that Floyd's killing represented another example of racist cops and the long history of racism in America. They made little mention that of the four officers involved and charged in Floyd's death, one officer is black and another is Asian American. Politicians and celebrities fell all over themselves apologizing for America's injustice to blacks and the deep roots of "systemic racism" in the police force. And, of course, anarchists groups like

Antifa used the ensuing peaceful protests as an excuse to riot, loot, burn stores, attack and harass cops, and beat up civilians all around the country. These riots injured and killed many people and cost Americans billions of dollars, at a time when many were already suffering from the impact of the Coronavirus lockdowns.

Despite the rarity of police shootings and absence of statistical proof they are not racially motivated, the Left has used the killing of George Floyd as an excuse to paint police as violent thugs "hunting" minorities. Many are now calling for police departments to be defunded and even disbanded. This is absurd! Police perform the most basic function of government: enforcing our laws and keeping our citizens safe from harm.

The lie that America is built on racism is a lie that perpetuates many social ills. We can't solve America's problems if we don't understand their real causes, and racism isn't the biggest by a long shot.

One of the problems with rooting out police brutality is often that police unions insulate their members from accountability. Public sector unions—whether of police, teachers, or Washington bureaucrats—make government workers less accountable to citizens and their elected representatives. That's a problem we could solve, except that government union bosses have historically been major donors and supporters of the Democrat Party. It is another reason leftists always prefer to talk about racism, as opposed to *doing* something about racism.

You want to see real racism? See the way Jews are treated across Europe and the Middle East. You want to see honest–to–God segregation? See the way the Chinese government treats Mongolians and Tibetans. Or do some research about the concentration camps the Chinese run to "re–educate" Muslim Uyghurs. Truly racist countries don't let their racial minorities protest!

Why They Lie

If everything the progressives want you to believe aboutAmerica's racial sins is false, what is their motivation for this big lie?

Once again, it's all about power. There is a reason the wokest of the woke are wealthy, privileged, and almost uniform—white, elites. The corporate, media, academic, and political establishment are the most powerful people in America. And they want to keep their power.

The American system and our traditional paradigm was built specifically to hold these powerful elites accountable—through free market competition, constitutional elections, political checks and balances, and our cultural emphasis on individual freedom over hierarchical power structures. That's why progressives want to discredit America and our traditional common–sense values. They do not want the accountability that comes with a free society. By making society less free, progressives can better secure their privilege.

That's really the goal: The Left wants to keep its power and control, period. And they know that they can use the "racist" attack to quickly discredit anyone. The Left knows if it can smear people who have different views, ideas, or arguments as "racist," however unfairly, they can bully their opponents and win their point.

That's one of the reasons progressives hate Donald Trump—unlike most Washington politicians of both parties, President Trump doesn't allow himself to be bullied. He fights back. Maybe that explains why, despite blanket media smears, candidate Trump in 2016 got more support from black and Latino voters than the supposedly more sympathetic and moderate Mitt Romney did in 2012.[45] Indeed, Trump won the election by winning the support of many of the voters who supported *Barack Obama* in 2008 and

2012. The media quickly brushed this story under the rug, because it doesn't fit the false narrative they need you to believe. Truth doesn't matter; just the prism.

That's why the progressive paradigm tells you, as in the 1619 Project, that *everything* is about slavery and race. Every public policy issue, every issue *period*, comes back to that one sin. It's a clever and effective trick. After all, if *everything* is about slavery and racism, and if woke progressives are the only ones who aren't racist, then everyone who opposes progressives about *anything* must therefore be a racist.

Just as progressives' opposition to religion isn't about God, progressives' emphasis on racism isn't about race—it's about *them*. They call America racist to fool or bully you into supporting their political ideas.

Progressives don't want you to merely oppose Donald Trump's message of "Make America Great Again." They need you to believe, in the words of New York Governor Andrew Cuomo, that "America was never that great."[46] But the facts of history are clear: America is not perfect, just heroic—and deserving of the love and gratitude that people all around the world have for her. On race, as on so many issues, America isn't the problem; America is the solution.

BIG LIE #3:
CLIMATE CHANGE IS THE
GREATEST THREAT TO MANKIND

"Climate change is a planetary crisis.
We have to act now, and we have to act boldly."
— Sen. Bernie Sanders (I–VT)[47]

"This is now about our industries, and governments around the
world taking decisive, large–scale action... The world's scientific
community has spoken, and they have given us our prognosis:
if we do not act together, we will surely perish."
— Leonardo DeCaprio[48]

The Lie:

Climate change caused by man–made CO_2 emissions will soon lead to irreversible ecological disaster.

The Facts:

- CO_2 levels only comprise 0.04% of Earth's atmosphere. Man–made carbon dioxide comprises about one–third of the Earth's CO_2, or just over one one–hundredth of one percent of the atmosphere.[49]

- A fact sheet issued by the Obama Administration's Environmental Protection Agency suggested that its proposed regulations to reduce carbon dioxide emissions at power plants would have prevented less than 0.02 degrees Celsius of global warming by 2100.[50]

- A 2020 study by federal researchers stated that "it is premature to conclude with high confidence that human activities—and particularly greenhouse gas emissions that cause global warming—have already had a detectable impact on hurricane activity."[51]
- In 2019, U.S. CO2 emissions fell by 2.9% compared to 2018 levels. American CO2 emissions now stand approximately 15% below 2000 levels, even as they continue to rise throughout the rest of the world.[52]

The Full Story

The climate has always changed. And it always will.

But are man–made carbon dioxide emissions causing disastrous, irreversible increases in global temperatures? No.

After decades of dire warnings of imminent destruction from climate change, none of the predictive models created by alarmists have come true.

In 1988, Philip Shabecoff at *The New York Times* reported that if the "buildup" of greenhouse gases was allowed to continue, "the effect is likely to be a warming of 3 to 9 degrees Fahrenheit [between now and] the years 2025 to 2050 . . . The rise in global temperature is predicted to ... cause[e] sea levels to rise by one to four feet by the middle of the next century."[53] Around the same time, the United Nations sounded the alarm that global warming would cause rising sea levels that would wash entire countries away by the year 2000.[54]

In his 2006 documentary *An Inconvenient Truth*, former Vice President Al Gore warned sea levels could rise 20 feet—a prediction Gore might now find inconvenient, as it has not materialized.[55] In 2009, then–British Prime Minister Gordon Brown predicted the world had only 50 days to save the planet from global warming.[56]

In 2012, Peter Wadhams, a professor of ocean physics at the University of Cambridge, predicted "global disaster" from the demise of the Arctic Sea in just four years.[57]

Not only have none of these dire predictions come to pass, but the lack of measurable increases in global temperatures caused many to admit global warming may have taken a "pause."[58]

By the beginning of the 21st century, some climate researchers began to question whether the Earth had actually warmed over the previous two decades. Their questions created desperation among leftists, who had counted on this issue to advance their global socialist agenda. Leftist interests inside and outside of government began to fund climate research to get the results they wanted.[59] Any researcher who questions or denies the existence of global warming will lose funding and be blacklisted by the scientific, media, and political elite.

Today, leftists blame climate change for heat waves, cold snaps, droughts, floods, hurricanes, earthquakes—nothing is exempt from the effects of climate change. Progressive politicians have proclaimed climate change an existential threat to mankind even though most climate models project a 1–2 degrees Celsius increase in global temperatures over the next fifty years. Based on past failures of climate modeling, even these modest projections of global increases in temperatures may not occur.

But these facts—particularly the relative stability of our climate today—have not stopped those on the progressive Left from claiming we are on the precipice of mass starvation and chaos. This dedication to political outcomes over objectivity threatens to undermine the seriousness with which we view the entire debate.[60]

Why They Lie

The Left's theological orthodoxy on climate change becomes clear when they condemn "climate deniers." "Denier" only has one other common context: crackpots who dispute Hitler's murder of six million Jews during World War II. This is not an accident. Climate change is so central to the leftist religion that apostasy triggers immediate comparisons to Nazis.

Why are we trying to transform the world's economic system— at a cost of trillions of dollars and millions of jobs—to eliminate fossil fuels, when the facts suggest that it will make almost no difference in CO_2 levels?[61] Common sense suggests that even dramatic decreases in man–made CO_2 likely will not cause measurable reductions in global temperatures for decades.[62] If nothing else, there are enough questions to warrant a civil debate.

The Left's solutions to climate change have one thing in common: They place more power in Washington and international organizations. The other thing they have in common is requiring a tremendous amount of sacrifice from regular Americans in return for negligible future gains. Look no further than the Green New Deal, proposed by Sen. Ed Markey (D–MA) and Rep. Alexandria Ocasio–Cortez (D–NY). Their proposal itself is light on details, but the accompanying "fact sheet" makes clear what the pair intend: a "massive transformation of our society."[63]

Among their proposals: the elimination of air travel, "retrofit[ting] every building in America," getting rid of cars with combustion engines, building "charging stations everywhere," and eradicating fossil fuels and nuclear energy sources entirely.[64]

But for Markey and Ocasio–Cortez, addressing climate change doesn't stop there. Their "transformational" package also includes government guaranteed jobs, free education, a house, a union, and free money for those "unwilling to work."[65] The Left doesn't just want to address climate change. They want to use the climate as an excuse to re-make your life, and use the government to do it.

The progressive Left isn't actually interested in improving the environment. As the data show, many of the societal transformations they are advocating would result in little to no reductions in real pollutants. But those transformations would lead to government control of everything from the car you drive, to the food you eat, to how you travel. And control is the name of the game.

BIG LIE #4:
WHITE PEOPLE
ARE ALL PRIVILEGED

"For those of us who work to raise the racial consciousness of whites, simply getting whites to acknowledge that our race gives us advantages is a major effort."
— **Robin DiAngelo**[66]

"You still have your whiteness. That's what the term 'white privilege' is. It means that whiteness still gives you an advantage, no matter."
— **Oprah Winfrey**[67]

The Lie:

Whites enjoy lifelong unearned advantages over people of other races.

The Facts:

• According to the Centers for Disease Control, white males committed nearly 7 out of 10 suicides in the United States in 2018.[68]

• According to the Census Bureau, Indian Americans, Pakistani Americans, Filipino Americans, Taiwanese Americans, Lebanese Americans, Sri Lankan Americans, Chinese Americans, and Iranian Americans all have higher median household incomes than non–Hispanic whites.[69]

- A 2014 Harvard study found family structure, not race, the top correlator of upward mobility.[70]
- Two-parent black families have a poverty rate of 7%, compared to a 22% poverty rate among white single-parent households.[71]
- In 2017, white men on average earned 80% of Asian men.[72]
- According to the Census Bureau, Asian Americans hold undergraduate, master's, and doctoral degrees at higher rates than whites. These disparities increase as educational levels rise, with Asian Americans holding doctoral degrees at more than twice the level of whites.[73]
- Thirty years after a generation of exiles left Cuba upon Fidel Castro's Communist takeover, second-generation Cuban Americans had yearly salaries exceeding $50,000 at twice the rate of whites. Today, Cuban American businesses generate more revenue than the entire island of Cuba.[74]
- More than two in three black high school graduates (70.9%) enrolled in college in 2013, several percentage points higher than whites' enrollment rate.[75]

The Full Story

Rather than soft-pedaling this one, let's just get the truth out in the open: white privilege is a crock... a lie. It's a scam, invented by (mostly white) progressive elites to protect *their own* privilege and power controlling the major institutions of American business, education, culture, media, and politics.

What is white privilege? A primer on the subject in the progressive *Yes!* magazine defined the term as "The reality that a white person's whiteness has come—and continues to come —with an array of benefits and advantages not shared by many people of color."[76]

Are there racists in America? Of course. Racists exist in every country around the world, because humanity is imperfect. A country of 330 million people will have some cranks and nuts of every stripe. Do African Americans still carry a burden because of slavery and old Jim Crow laws? Of course. But the idea that those two facts can be thrown into a blender and mixed up to produce a uniform, universal "privilege" enjoyed by all white Americans at the expense of all black or brown Americans is simply false.

It's not simply false as a moral assertion. It's empirically false. It's demonstrably false. It's a meaningless slur designed by progressives to invalidate their critics. It's nonsense.

America is one of the least racist, most diverse countries on Earth!

Here are the facts.

Privileges of all kinds—advantages that people are born with and did nothing to earn—are everywhere.

A young basketball player who grows to seven feet tall will enjoy physical and athletic advantages that an equally talented six-foot player does not. It doesn't matter how hard the shorter player works; he or she will have a hard time competing with the giant. Shaquille O'Neal and Larry Bird worked their tails off to become NBA legends, but their *heights*—7'1" and 6'9"—had nothing to do with either their talent or their work ethic. They were privileged to be tall. Had they reached only the average height for an American male—five-foot-nine-inches—in all likelihood they would have become no more than good pickup players at their local YMCA.

In the same way, go stand next to an NFL football player and tell me the difference between him and you is just a few hours at the gym. Think of all the really good high school athletes never recruited to play at big time colleges, let alone have a crack at the pros. Now have you ever heard someone complain about "Might Privilege"? Or is this just one of the million ways that, as my Mom used to say, "life ain't fair?"

But forget about sports. Look where else we see vast chasms of unequal opportunities in huge swaths of our society.

You know who else enjoys unearned privileges throughout their lives? Kids whose parents got married and stayed married. Kids whose parents took them to church every week. Kids whose parents were not addicted to drugs and alcohol. Kids whose parents read books—and specifically read books to them.

In every instance, these variables have *nothing* to do with a child's own decisions, virtues or vices. It's literally just part of the hand of cards they were dealt at the beginning of the game. And lest there be any doubt, life has worked this way for every generation of every human society in the history of the world since the dawn of time.

Ah, you might say, but those things are *just matters* of luck. White privilege is a comprehensive system of advantage and disadvantage that follows people of different races throughout their lives, *always* cutting in favor of white children and adults and against black children and adults. White privilege may be *populated* by chance, but it is perpetuated by choice.

Do you believe that life is just easier for all white people? Do Appalachian towns—mostly populated by whites—hollowed out by closed coal mines and outsourced jobs and now beset by a deadly opioid crisis look like bastions of "privilege?"

It is true that average, white Americans have better educational attainment than blacks and Latinos. But if that is the result of "white privilege," then why do Asian Americans have better educational attainment than whites? Is it because of racism and social injustice, or because of better performance in school or family support structures?

The American higher education system gives many racial preferences, which cut *against* white students and Asian students, in favor of other minorities like black and Latino Americans. If three students with identical grades, test scores, and extracurricular achievements—one Asian American, one white, and one black— all apply to a college seeking to fill minority quotas, the black student will have the "privilege," for literally no reason other than the color of his or her skin.

It's the same logic by which Sen. Elizabeth Warren (D–MA) pretended to be a Native American when she told the Texas State Bar and her employers at Harvard that she was a Cherokee Indian and not the Caucasian she really is.[77] It has nothing to do with her 1/1000th genetic heritage.[78] She exploited the diversity–fetishists who run the legal profession and the elite academy. She guessed, rightly, that suddenly becoming a "woman of color" would *help* her career.

The real truth, backed up by mountains of data, is this: what separates the haves from the have–nots in America today isn't race, it's defining life choices like marriage and hard work. If a young American graduates high school, gets a full time job, gets married and then has kids—*in that order*—his or her chances of winding up in poverty are miniscule. There is no moral judgment in this "Success Sequence"—it's common sense. It's what every parent wants for their kids. It's what most children would *say* they want out of life.

The principles behind this "Success Sequence" only sound revolutionary to the progressive Left. Saving money is harder than spending it—but it's how you accumulate wealth. Studying is harder than partying—but it's how you get an education. Hustling is harder than goofing off at your job—but that's how you get raises and promotions. Getting married is more demanding than staying single, and staying married is harder than breaking up—

but that's how you provide the most and best opportunities for your children. Going to church on Sunday is harder than sleeping in—but it's how you get yourself right with God and, more often than not, with everyone else. The principles of success not only follow common sense, they are backed up by more research than you would ever want to read.

First generation Americans are often poor, under-educated immigrants, who arrive penniless but, through courage and determination, make their way into the working class. *Their* kids do a little better: they finish high school, learn a trade, maybe go to college and own a home, and make their way into the middle class. Their kids go to better schools, graduate from college, inherit a little nest egg from mom and dad, and aim ever higher. Over generations, immigrants from all over the world—white, black, Latino, Asian, you name it—have come here and achieved that same success story.

It is easier to achieve in America than anywhere in the world. But it's still really hard. And while it can take a family three generations and 50 years or more to build up a prosperous, thriving life... one generation can tear it all down in the blink of an eye. One drug or gambling addiction, one divorce, one night of drunk driving or infidelity, one violent outburst or incurable diagnosis, one untimely death, one failed business investment, and it can all come crashing down—no matter what color your skin is.

And no matter what your skin color is, you will enjoy the benefits and bear the burdens your parents hand you. You played no part in their success or their failure, their virtues or their vices, their own good luck or bad luck, their good decisions or their bad ones.

That's not perfect, and it may not even be fair; it's just a fact of life.

Why They Lie

Author and radio talk show host Dennis Prager explains why the Left needs victims:

> So then why all this left-wing talk about white privilege? The major reason is in order to portray blacks as victims. This achieves two huge goals for the Left—one political, the other philosophical.
>
> The political goal is to ensure that blacks continue to view America as racist. The Left knows that the only way to retain political power in America is to perpetuate the belief among black Americans that their primary problem is white racism. Only then will blacks continue to regard the Left and the Democrats as indispensable.[79]
>
> The philosophical reason is that the Left denies—as it has since Marx—the primacy of moral and cultural values in determining the fate of the individual and of society. In the Left's view, it is not poor values or a lack of moral self-control that causes crime, but poverty and, in the case of black criminals, racism. Therefore, the disproportionate amount of violent crime committed by black males is not attributable to the moral failure of the black criminal or to the likelihood of his not having been raised by a father, but to an external factor over which he has little or no power—white racism.

"White privilege" serves the same "original sin" purpose as "climate change"—it's a pervasive, universal reality that no one can ever be redeemed through their own merits. Redemption can only be gained through the ministrations of the one true faith of our elite institutional establishment: progressive politics.

These elites use the "white privilege" lie—and ubiquitous, dishonest accusations of racism against their political opponents—to preserve and grow their power. And it works. Government grows larger and larger every year. Our leading political, cultural, and academic institutions grow more "woke" every day, yet somehow, for all their supposed valiant social justice warring, the invisible "white privilege" bogeyman remains as large and menacing as ever.

In reality, "white privilege" is a made-up excuse to distract people from the fact the promised benefits of progressive government *never actually arrive.* The only people benefiting from "white privilege" are the rich, mostly white, progressive elites who cooked up the whole idea.

And for all the unfair animosity it stokes toward white Americans, its true victims are the less affluent black families and communities that leftist elites feed the self-defeating premise that they cannot succeed in life. African American writer John McWhorter attacked the "dehumanizing condescension" of *White Fragility*—both the book by Robin DiAngelo and the premise behind it:

> Despite the sincere intentions of its author, the book diminishes black people in the name of dignifying us.... Few books have more openly infantilized black people than this supposedly authoritative tome....DiAngelo's outlook rests upon a depiction of black people as endlessly delicate poster children within this self-gratifying fantasy about how America needs to think—or, better, stop thinking. Her answer to white fragility, in other words, entails an elaborate and pitilessly dehumanizing condescension toward black people.[80]

Almost every American today, of every race, does indeed judge their neighbor by the content of their character, not the color of their skin. Success is available to all Americans. It is also difficult to attain, and always extremely fragile. It's not easy, but it's easier today in the United States than it has ever been at any other time or in any other place in the history of mankind.

Opportunities expand for everyone when we have lots of choices of friends, schools, jobs, places to live, entertainment, food, clothes and what we believe and say. The more choices, the more freedom—and the more freedom, the more opportunities for everyone.

But ultimately, opportunities don't create success. People do. That's why every American needs the character, skills, and drive to succeed in a free society. Your race is not an impediment to success in America; believing that it is, however, will kill your chances of success.

BIG LIE #5:
AMERICAN WOMEN
ARE DISADVANTAGED

*"The hard truth is women—and particularly women of color—
have never had a fair shot to get ahead in this country."*
— Vice President Joe Biden[81]

*"Sexism exerts its pull on our politics and our society every day,
in ways both subtle and crystal clear."*
— Sen. Hillary Clinton (D–NY)[82]

The Lie:

Women are held back by rampant sexism in American society,
which prevents them from attaining equal pay and powerful jobs.

The Truth:

- Data compiled by multiple employer databases in multiple
  countries indicate that when comparing men and women in the
  same jobs, with the same experience, working the same amount
  of hours, the gender pay gap virtually disappears.[83]

- A Harvard University study found that the small gender
  pay gaps that do exist are explained largely by different
  lifestyle choices, such as women preferring more predictable
  working hours.[84]

- The percentage of businesses majority–owned by women
  grew from 4.6% in 1972 to 42% in 2019. Women are also more
  likely to start a business than men.[85]

- In 1970, 14.1% of men and 8.2% of women over age 25 held at least a Bachelor's degree. By 2019, a greater percentage of women (36.6%) than men (35.4%) held at least a Bachelor's degree.[86]
- According to the federal Department of Education, women currently comprise:
  - 49.3% of all faculty at degree–granting colleges and universities;
  - 56.6% of all students enrolled in four–year undergraduate colleges and universities;
  - 57.2% of all the Bachelor's degrees awarded;
  - 59.3% of all the Master's degrees awarded; and
  - 53.3% of all the doctoral degrees awarded.[87]
- The number of female medical school enrollees, both in absolute terms and as a percentage of overall enrollment, has steadily risen over the past four decades, such that women now represent a majority (52.4%) of medical school students.[88]

The Full Story

When I first heard about the Equal Rights Amendment as a teenager, I thought, "This is great! Men will finally get a fair chance."

My first notion of women was shaped by one of the meanest, toughest, hardest working and successful persons I have ever known—my mother. I don't think she ever met a man who didn't fear her. So it never occurred to me that women were disadvantaged in any way.

Betty Rawlings grew up before and during World War II. There were few sports teams for young girls, but somehow my mother knew how to throw and kick a football, swing a baseball bat, and shoot a basketball. I know because she taught me. She was a beauty queen in high school, but kept a large tool box at our home and knew how to fix just about anything.

Betty married a dashing young Air Force pilot, Tom DeMint, who had come home from the war. They had four children in less than six years, but soon divorced. With no job or child support, my mother had no income and four children to feed.

The job market for women at the time consisted mostly of teaching, nursing, and secretarial work. But none of this worked for a mom who needed to stay at home to take care of four kids. So Betty started the DeMint Academy of Dance and Decorum—in our home. We spent a day knocking down the wall between the living room and dining room, and installed black and white linoleum squares on the floor to create a ballroom.

Betty first served the kids in our neighborhood, but after pitching her service to several local high school principals, she bought a 1959 Volkswagen bus and began picking up teenagers after school and bringing them back to our home for lessons in dance and decorum. Betty then got their parents interested, and soon began hosting adult classes in our home every night.

Betty DeMint became a local celebrity. For many in Greenville, South Carolina, it became a "rite of passage" to graduate from her academy. I still meet people all around the country who call her classes a major factor in their success.

Betty later remarried Johnny Batson, a local radio celebrity, and moved to Hilton Head, South Carolina. She became a real estate agent, started Batson Brokerage, and soon became the top salesperson on the island for seven years in a row. All this from a single mom who never graduated college!

Many more women today work hard like my mother, but unfortunately, many more men have shunned their roles of service and leadership.

When I was a businessman providing market research and strategic planning for organizations and companies, I volunteered to help a local charity develop strategies for community leadership in government housing projects. We held a series of focus groups with residents to determine how we could encourage self–governance and individual leadership. I was stunned at how few men were present in these communities. The social workers called them matriarchal communities. By default, women—primarily single mothers and grandmothers—led these communities.

These heroic mothers and grandmothers raised the children until many of the boys became uncontrollable as teenagers. Many of the boys dropped out of high school. Some became fathers in their teens. Some got wrapped up with the wrong crowd, ended up using drugs, or ran into trouble with the law. It previewed what has happened with boys and men of all backgrounds in America. The percentage of college–educated men working in high–wage cognitive occupations continues to fall, even as the percentage for women keeps rising.[89]

This decline of men is being fed by a progressive campaign that is destroying the traditional role of men in the family and society. Traditionally, boys in America grew up believing they would provide for and lead their families. But progressives define "leading" as men controlling and dominating women. According to progressives, anyone who believes in men's traditional role is a chauvinist.

Unfortunately, the Left has continuously maligned the traditional role of men in America for decades. Women don't need men to be their providers and protectors, and couples don't need to be married to have sex and children. As presented by progressives, men have no special roles or responsibilities in society, except to serve themselves. Under this view, everyone—men and women—should live to satisfy their own needs and do whatever makes them feel good.

But for men, forgoing their leadership role in the family, business, and community often leads to dysfunction and depression.[90]

Unfortunately, current trends suggest the decline of men, and the corresponding societal problems, will get worse in the future. Although males comprise roughly half of the population, they make up 56% of high school dropouts.[91] And for young men, dropping out of high school often means a lifetime of poverty, drugs, and crime.

A 2009 study concluded that nearly one in ten (9.4%) young male high school dropouts is in jail or juvenile detention, compared with only one in 500 (0.2%) young male college graduates.[92] The picture is even worse for African Americans, as a Brookings Institution study found that an African American male dropout had a nearly 70% chance of being imprisoned by age 35.[93]

Life for American women is not one long cake walk. But life is hard *for everyone*. And over the last few decades, while women have made demonstrable—in some cases, astronomical—gains in every part of American society, life has been getting harder and harder for men.

Why They Lie

The progressive goal is to dismantle traditional values and roles in society. They wish to replace the essential building blocks of society—marriage, family, volunteer organizations, churches, local schools, small businesses, communities—with distant government bureaucracies they can control.

The constant progressive chorus about America's injustice to women accomplishes the same goals as their chorus about racism—to enfeeble you and empower themselves. If you believe the deck is unfairly stacked against you, you're more likely to believe you can't overcome life's obstacles without government's help.

The progressive paradigm not only blinds us with lies, it obscures America's real problems. The truth is that women are moving ahead in America and men are falling behind. Many of America's problems—crime, drugs, incarcerations, homelessness, suicides, and poor health—are linked to fatherless homes and the dire situation of American men.

BIG LIE #6:
CAPITALISM ONLY WORKS
FOR THE GREEDY RICH

"Capitalism is an ideology of capital—the most important
thing is the concentration of capital and to seek and
maximize profit. To me, capitalism is irredeemable."
— **Rep. Alexandria Ocasio–Cortez (D–NY)**[94]

"It's time for an economic revolution.
Capitalism today is failing us, killing us,
and robbing from our children's future."
— **Mark Ruffalo, actor**[95]

The Lie:

Capitalism is an oppressive economic system designed to help
the rich and hurt the poor.

The Facts:

- A 2009 study concluded that from 1970 to 2006, the number of
  people in poverty fell around the world by more than half, from
  403 million to 152 million. The number of people in poverty
  fell even as the global population rose, meaning that the poverty
  rate declined by 80%.[96]

- The same study suggests a strong link between capitalism and
  falling poverty. In 1970, the East Asian region—which includes
  "Asian Tigers" like Hong Kong, Singapore, Taiwan, and South
  Korea—had 58.8% of its people in poverty—the most of

any region. By 2006, only 1.7% of East Asian people lived in poverty—the lowest of any region.[97]

- Capitalism has provided material wealth beyond what prior generations could have imagined, even for those in poverty in the United States. For instance, a 2013 Census Bureau report found that overwhelming majorities of those under the poverty line in America have access to a refrigerator (97.8%), stove (96.6%), television (96.1%), microwave (93.2%), air conditioner (83.4%), cell phone (80.9%), and satisfactory housing (93.3%).[98]

- Data from the World Bank and federal Bureau of Economic Analysis indicate that on a consumption basis, the poorest 20% of Americans consume more goods and services than the average consumption of people of *all* incomes in prosperous western countries like the United Kingdom, Japan, Sweden, Australia, and Canada.[99]

- The World Bank has set a poverty level of $1.90 per day, or less than $700 per year. An American making the federal minimum wage ($7.25 per hour) exceeds the World Bank's annual poverty threshold by working 95.7 hours, or less than three full weeks per year.[100]

- While the Left continually attacks capitalism, Americans prefer it to the alternatives. According to a 2019 Pew Research poll, nearly two-thirds (65%) of Americans have a positive view of capitalism, with only 33% negative. By comparison, a majority (55%) of Americans think negatively of socialism, with only 42% responding positively.[101]

- The Pew poll also found that a majority of Democrats think favorably of capitalism (55%). Another survey found that even among Americans with incomes under $20,000, as many supported capitalism (49%) as socialism (49%).[102]

The Full Story

There are so many lies about capitalism that it's impossible to keep up with them all. *Capitalism exploits workers. Capitalism rewards oppression and cruelty. It sucks the humanity from people by turning us into wage slaves. Capitalism doesn't create wealth; it just allows rich to steal it from everyone else. Capitalism destroys the environment.* But all these lies about capitalism all spring from one big lie at the root of all these complaints: *Capitalism only benefits greedy rich people.*

This lie is so dumb, so ahistorical, so false in theory and in practice that it's hard to think anyone actually believes it. But as we'll find out, they really don't.

People who *think* they hate capitalism either don't understand what capitalism is, or are just lying to themselves.

In truth, *everyone* is a capitalist. Deep down, all of us want the freedom to buy and sell things we want at prices we decide are fair. The big difference between capitalism and socialism is the difference between spending our *own money* the way we choose, or having someone else choose to spend *our* money they way *they* choose.

The progressive propaganda machine has told us that a socialist economic system holds wealth in common, and shares it with everyone equally. Sounds fair enough, right? Except it's been tried all over the world for centuries, and it never works out that way. Socialist leaders promise equality, and instead deliver corruption and poverty—wealth for the politically connected and suffering for everyone else. In the real world, socialism just becomes crony capitalism run amok for high government officials—with the rest of us working as indentured servants for their benefit.

Sorry to burst your bubble, but unless you are an ordained

monk who has taken a vow of poverty, deep down you are most likely either a hard–core capitalist ... or you're a thief. Let's find out which!

Before we determine whether you are a capitalist or a criminal, let's clarify what we're talking about. What is capitalism, after all?

If you like, you can read whole libraries of books explaining capitalism down to the tiniest details. But at the basic level, capitalism is incredibly simple. For all the complexities of Wall Street, the Federal Reserve, the confusing math and vocabulary of economics, it comes down to this: under capitalism people are free to buy what they want and sell the things they create, charging or paying whatever price the buyers and sellers agree.

The idea that capitalism is for greedy rich people is completely upside down. *Feudalism,* the economic system in Europe during the Middle Ages, forced the poor and working classes to serve the rich. Capitalism does something more like the opposite. It forces even wealthy people to *earn* their revenue, usually from people much less wealthy than themselves.

Ray Kroc, the man who made McDonald's a household name, always reminded his senior managers that he—the CEO—was *not* in charge of the McDonalds's menu—the customers were. If he wanted the restaurants to succeed, he needed to give people what they wanted. In a capitalist economy, and *only* in a capitalist economy, *the people* decide which goods, services, and businesses succeed and which fail.

For instance, Netflix didn't put Blockbuster Video out of business —consumers did, by choosing to spend their money on streaming movies at home rather than driving across town to rent DVDs.

Why? Because in a capitalist system, *we're all capitalists.* Sometimes we're buyers, and sometimes we're sellers. Most regularly, we sell our labor, for which our employers pay us.

Progressives want you to believe that capitalism is this foreign, alien thing being done *to* you—not *by* you, but by "the 1%" or "the

Big Banks" or other greedy rich people. They want you to resent the fact that some people—probably lots of people—have more money than you.

Well, sure, lots of people have more money than you. LeBron James and Michael Jordan have more money than you because they're two of the greatest athletes of all time, and basketball fans happily spend a ton of time and money watching their games, buying their branded products, and on and on. Nobody's walking around my hometown in South Carolina with a "DeMint" jersey (well, maybe an old campaign T-shirt they got for free).

The final, most important point about capitalism is this: it works. It's not just a theory—it's been affirmed by centuries of history. There is a reason that capitalist-oriented countries like the United States go from poor to rich and socialist countries like Cuba and Venezuela go from rich to poor. It's not luck.

But if capitalism is so great, why are many people—from the media, to college professors, to Hollywood celebrities and the progressive Left—so enamored with socialism?

Let's pose the same question we asked about capitalism. What is socialism? In one sense, socialism is capitalism's opposite. Instead of individuals owning their own property, and buying and selling things as they see fit, the government owns or controls all the property. Socialists usually don't put it quite this way. They say they want society to own things together in partnership. That actually sounds nice, doesn't it?

As a Christian, I certainly believe in being sociable and sharing with others! Socialism sounds ... well, social. It sounds nice and generous. It claims to replace the risk and inequality of free markets with security and equality. It appeals to our instincts of "sharing" and "compassion."

Sound too good to be true? Well, it is.

Authoritarian philosophies like socialism and communism are based on two core assumptions, both false.

For starters, these systems assume that a permanent, greedy, mean, infinite tangible stock of "wealth of the rich" sits in a vault somewhere, just waiting for a Robin Hood government with the courage and wisdom to seize it and divide all the riches among everyone.

But that's idiotic. Rich people don't act like Scrooge McDuck, swimming laps in a giant pool of gold coins. That pool doesn't exist. Wealth has to be created one piece of gold at a time. Except for the very old, the very young, the disabled, or just plain lazy, all the rest of us are working, creating wealth—little by little— every day through hard work and perseverance, blood, sweat, and tears.

And once someone has climbed to the mountaintop of success, most don't hoard their fortunes while sneering at the destitute. Exactly the opposite, in fact: The wealthy are more likely to donate to charities. In fact, the top 1% (those making about $400,000 or more) provide about one-third of all charitable donations, and the wealthiest 1.4% of Americans provide 86% of the charitable bequests made at death.[103]

The second false assumption at the core of socialism is that there

are wise, honest, and quasi-angelic people who, given the power to spend *everyone else's* money, will do so selflessly and efficiently in ways that benefit everybody. But that's never happened. In any country. Ever. Not once. Not even for a few weeks at a time.

Everywhere socialism has been tried, it has made government officials fantastically rich, and everyone else poor. Once you centralize economic power, you centralize *political* power, and once you centralize both, corruption follows sure as night follows day. Every communist dictator in the world has lived in opulent luxury. Fidel Castro first came to power as a peasant revolutionary; after ruling for decades as a murderous tyrant over a starving nation, he died with an estimated net worth of nearly $1 billion.[104] North Korea's communist leader Kim Jong Un? Also a billionaire.[105] So was Venezuelan socialist leader Hugo Chavez, whose daughter is now the wealthiest person in Venezuela.[106] By some accounts, Russian strongman Vladimir Putin is estimated to be wealthiest man on the planet.[107]

These bad apples don't just exist elsewhere around the world. Even in the U.S., we can see the beginnings of similar corruption. Six of the ten wealthiest counties in America are suburbs of Washington, D.C., a city with no significant manufacturing or industry, and whose only real "business" consists of political influence peddling.[108] Talk about "privilege."

The basic building blocks that make capitalism possible are also critical to human flourishing: free trade, property rights, the rule of law, and judicial oversight. You can't buy and sell things without property rights, meaning there's no point in creating or buying something if the government or thieves can just take it from you. And property rights wouldn't be worth much without a system of law and order to enforce them: a police force to stop the criminals from stealing what you work for, and a judicial system to apply the law fairly and enact justice.

Talk to any charity or missionary fighting oppression around the world and they will tell you that tyrannical countries lack these basic concepts of capitalism, fairness, and justice under the law.

Karl Marx wrote in *The Communist Manifesto*: "The theory of communism may be summed up in one sentence: abolish all private property." But if you don't own your house, your car, your phone, then who does? The government, of course. And if you believe all governments will be run by angels with perfect wisdom, that might make sense. But as James Madison famously noted in *Federalist No. 51*, "If men were angels, no government would be necessary." Madison recognized that power corrupts humans, making citizens without private property simply slaves to the state.

This is why America's Framers gave the power to the people, not to a King. This is why we call America exceptional. This is why America has inspired those yearning for freedom around the world for centuries.

America's example of free market capitalism has not only lifted millions of our own people of out of poverty, it has lifted billions out of poverty worldwide. Capitalism allows the accumulation of wealth that funds charities and government programs, and affords the poor the opportunity to climb up the economic ladder.

Socialism in practice isn't the utopia of John Lennon's "Imagine." It's more like the dystopia of Suzanne Collins' *Hunger Games* books, where a capital of government-connected elites steal the wealth created by the rest of the country.

Socialism isn't the opposite of capitalism. It's just a corrupted, exclusive form of it—untold power and wealth for the select elite who run the government and big institutions, and powerlessness for everyone else.

In a socialist system, rich and powerful government officials can

buy what they want, sell what they want, at prices *they* deem appropriate, while denying that same right to everyone else. Consumers can't customize their priorities—they have to take what government experts decide is right for them.

Socialist leaders are every bit as capitalist as everyone else. They just don't think the rest of us are smart and virtuous enough to have that power, and so they want to take our property away from us and control it as *they* see fit.

Why They Lie

In progressives' upside–down world, the capitalists, who only want to spend their own money, get called greedy, while the socialists who want to spend *everyone else's* money are supposedly the selfless ones.

The challenge for conservatives trying to preserve capitalism

and the prosperity it brings is that socialism sounds so much easier—"Just let the government do it." It is the constant refrain from the Left, whether the issue is health care, education, environment, transportation, banking, or in the case of socialism, the entire economy. When it comes to the sales pitch for socialists, progressives are essentially giving away free candy. It sounds incredibly appealing—but only to those who don't know how prosperity is created.

It is indeed terrible when those who amass wealth can bend government policy to privilege themselves at the expense of everyone else. But that's not capitalism: that's crony capitalism with a lot of corruption. The free market absolutely depends on the rule of law and the equal rights of all citizens. That is why conservatives are suspicious of big government. The more control government has over the economy, the more opportunities special interests have to twist the writing and enforcing of laws to suit their interests.

That is why people in D.C. have become so rich as the government has gotten so big. Those who work in and around the Capitol always end up snorting up a nice percentage of federal spending, and so Washington insiders have become a special interest all to themselves—continuously pushing America away from capitalism and toward socialism. To Washington elites, socialism is just a higher form of capitalism—where the "capital" is everyone else's money.

Real capitalism threatens the politicians and the elite because it decentralizes power and reduces their ability to control society. That is precisely why so many elites *hate* the free enterprise system. They believe *they* should be in charge. Capitalism, individual property rights, and the rule of law prevent them from ruling society from above.

Capitalism, like any man–made system, is far from perfect. But the forces of free markets, when paired with the mediating influence of religious virtue and minimal government regulation, has done more to create prosperity and opportunities than any other economic system in history.

Free market capitalism has lifted billions of people out of poverty all around the world—far more than any government program ever could.

BIG LIE #7:
BIG GOVERNMENT
HELPS THE POOR

"Republicans want smaller government
for the same reason crooks want fewer cops:
It's easier to get away with murder."
— James Carville[109]

"This administration here and now
declares an unconditional war on poverty."
— President Lyndon Johnson[110]

The Lie:

Massive federal programs provide essential services and lift Americans out of poverty.

The Facts:

- The "War on Poverty" initiated by Lyndon Johnson in 1964 has cost taxpayers $22 trillion, with little in the way of measurable success. Adjusted for inflation, these programs have cost three times as much as every American war, from the War for Independence to the present.[111]

- Public housing projects exacerbate poverty rather than relieving it, creating generational poverty by concentrating single parenthood, crime, poor academic performance, and other social ills in certain neighborhoods and communities.[112]

- In the ten years after a Republican Congress enacted the 1996 welfare reform law, the number of welfare recipients fell by 56%, employment rose rapidly among single mothers, and the child poverty rate declined, lifting 1.6 million children out of poverty.[113]

- After over $180 billion spent on the Head Start program over nearly half a century, a 2012 study concluded that non–Head Start students are more prepared in math skills than those who participated in the program.[114]

- Upward mobility in America has slowed down since the advent of the federal welfare state. While 90% of American children born in 1940 earned more than their parents at the same age, that number declined to about 50% for kids born in the 1980s.[115]

The Full Story

The lie that capitalism hurts poor people is even more harmful given the Left's solution: big government—the only way the Left believes we can lift people out of poverty.

For generations, progressives have described politics as a simple tug-of-war between the forces of rich, selfish, heartless, closed-minded, blood-sucking corporate stooges, and – on the other side, the kind, generous, tolerant, open-minded, and open-hearted people who will use government to help the little guy.

Four decades ago, conservatives resisted the creation of the federal Department of Education and, before that, the American Left's promotion of federal welfare programs to "help" the poor for many reasons. Advocates of limited government argued against the cost of such programs, their constitutionality, and the danger that such poorly designed plans would ultimately harm the people they were supposed to benefit. These concerns proved well-founded.

Conservatives who still make these points today are either ignored or attacked—for their heartless cruelty, their unfeeling penny-pinching, and for trying to "balance the budget on the backs of the poor."

As a result, many senators and representatives find it easier just to vote for *all the spending*, ignore their oversight responsibilities, and leave the problems for someone else to clean up. And so, year after year, Congress funnels more and more money into these programs that not only don't help, but which affirmatively harm poor and working-class families.

Take one of the most universal social services government provides in the United States: primary and secondary education. It serves as a good example of how badly government provides even the most basic services to the public.

The most recent data for math and reading achievement for 12th graders on the National Assessment of Educational Progress (NAEP) demonstrate just how poorly most American students fare. According to the data, just 25% of 12th graders achieved proficiency in math, and only 37% were proficient in reading.[116] Worryingly, the percentage of 12th graders performing below basic proficiency in math and reading rose on the 2015 test compared to the 2013 tests—a deterioration of 10% on both counts.[117] Average 12th grade reading scores actually declined from 1992 through 2015.[118]

In fact, the NAEP's long-term assessment finds today's high school seniors perform no better in reading than the high school seniors of the early 1970s.[119] Moreover, disparities between white and black students have not improved in years, and in many cases decades. In subject after subject—from civics, economics, geography, and American history to math and science—the gap between 12th grade African American and white students has not statistically improved.[120] In reading, black–white disparities among 12th graders increased from 1992 to 2015.[121]

These continued failings take place against the backdrop of spending per pupil which, after adjusting for inflation, continues to rise ever higher. Public expenditures on elementary and secondary schools totaled $707.6 billion in 2016–17, and averaged $13,010 per student in K–12 public education— a level of per–pupil spending that exceeds what many private schools charge.[122]

Over the past thirty years, spending on a per–pupil basis has grown by 41.7% *after accounting for inflation*.[123] Have public schools gotten 41.7% better in the past thirty years to justify this additional spending? Hardly. So where does the money go?

Some of the massive increase in spending went to teachers, but most went to non–teaching staff and administration. Between the 1970 and 2017 school years, the number of students in public schools increased by 11.1%.[124] But the number of public school teachers during the same period increased by 57.2%.[125] Non–teaching staff—central office bureaucracy—increased by a stunning 151%.[126]

Even though teachers now comprise less than half (48.4%) of all public–education employees, we have more teachers teaching fewer students than at any point in history.[127] The student–teacher ratio—that is, the number of students per full–time teacher in a given school—remains near all–time low levels.[128] Smaller class sizes are supposed to help students, but they haven't.

The money supposed to help underprivileged students achieve a better life actually helps the lives of the middlemen—the lobbyists and special interests, the bureaucrats and administrators, the teachers' unions and the politicians. At every turn, the less fortunate—poor students, poor neighborhoods, poor minority communities—get left behind, while affluent and well-connected elites ride the government gravy train.

There is a better way. All around the country, more education choices—public and private—have improved education outcomes for all students, especially poor and at risk children. We know government run schools have not helped the poor. Isn't it time we give parents and children more choices?

While private school costs per student are frequently comparable to or lower than public schools, homeschooling can cost a fraction of per-pupil spending on public education, often less than $1,000 a year. Yet private and homeschooling students routinely have higher average ACT and SAT scores than their public school counterparts.[129]

The welfare system proper—that is, federal programs specifically designed to redistribute resources to the poor—are even less effective than our government-run education system.

For the most part, the poverty rate goes down when the economy grows and creates jobs, and rises when the economy contracts during recessions. Good economies lift people out of poverty, not government welfare. Considering the ups and downs of the economy, the poverty rate in America is essentially unchanged, going no lower than 11.1% and no higher than 15.2% over the past half-century.[130]

This stagnation in the poverty rate comes despite the massive expenditures at the federal, state, and local levels to fight poverty. What are we doing wrong? There was a time when Americans opposed welfare because they feared it would reward freeloading. "We can't let the safety net become a hammock!" politicians would say in stump speeches.

But the real tragedy of America's welfare system is not that it rewards idleness. It's that these well–meaning welfare programs actually punish employment. Work is—and always has been—the *only* sustainable way for people to escape poverty. The safety net isn't becoming a hammock; it has become a trap, a snare the government throws over poor people that holds them down.

In fact, Gene Steuerle of the Urban Institute has called our welfare system exactly that: a "poverty trap."[131] The complicated system of means–tested welfare benefits means that, if their income rises, poor and near–poor families will lose almost as much in benefits as they gain in additional income.

The Congressional Budget Office noted that Obamacare would discourage work, reducing the labor supply by the equivalent of 2.5 million full–time jobs.[132] But the federal policies that discourage work preceded Obamacare, and go well beyond it. A recent study concluded that "one in four of our poorest households, regardless of age, make between two and three times as much from the government when they don't work than they make when they earn an extra $1,000 from working."[133] That's not just terrible policymaking, it's destructive, period. And it's obviously not working.

Medicaid, the massive federal–state program to provide health insurance for lower income Americans, costs Washington over $400 billion a year—more than six times the approximately $60 billion the federal government spends annually on K–12 education.[134] Giving health care to those Americans who can't afford it provides an essential service, right? Well, a groundbreaking *New England Journal of Medicine* study in 2013 found no significant improvements in physical health outcomes between those enrolled in Medicaid and the uninsured.[135] In other words, you'd likely be no healthier on Medicaid than with no health insurance at all.

The Veterans Affairs health care service, also run by the federal government, had a notorious reputation for bad service and long wait times for care well before the 2014 scandal exposed systemic corruption, mismanagement, and lethal incompetence.[136]

We've spent countless billions on public housing, yet the unsheltered homeless population grew by more than 20% over the last five years![137] We've spent tens of trillions of dollars and created hundreds of government welfare programs since Lyndon Johnson's War on Poverty of the 1960s, yet all that spending hasn't had much impact on either homelessness or poverty.

Why They Lie

Everywhere the federal government steps in to "help" lower income Americans, their lives get worse: their schools, their health care, their housing, their neighborhoods. The Left says government employee unions will help; they hurt. They say more spending on welfare will help; it hurts. They say more federal programs will help; they don't.

Look at the unrest across the country in 2020 following the killing of George Floyd. The cities that saw the worst violence and most vehement protests—Minneapolis, Chicago, Seattle, Atlanta, Washington D.C.—where demonstrators demanded an end to failed, discriminatory policies, all had Democratic mayors and city councils for decades—demonstrable proof of the Left's failed policies.

The Left insists their side has the answers to cure poverty, yet even after $22 trillion from Congress, the poor still live where their streets aren't safe, their schools are substandard, their health coverage makes them no healthier, and their welfare programs trap them in poverty.

If you worry about the plight of the poor, compare the success of free enterprise in lifting people out of poverty to the welfare state's miserable, wasteful, demonstrable failure. Consider the possibility that these systems enrich another class of people: the permanent bureaucracy, union bosses, Washington politicians, advocates and activists, and all those whose careers depend on the Poverty, Inc. millwheels to keep grinding.

BIG LIE #8:
OPEN BORDERS
ARE COMPASSIONATE

*"The kind of [border] wall that is proposed now
is a monument to hate and division.
We are a better country than that."*
— Sen. Elizabeth Warren (D–MA)[138]

"An undocumented immigrant is not a criminal."
— Sen. Kamala Harris (D–CA)[139]

*"Our plan treats the protection of refugees as the
objective and national borders as the obstacle."*
— George Soros[140]

The Lie:

Looser immigration restrictions and border enforcement are good
for America.

The Facts:

- A Harvard economist found that immigration lowers wages for
  low–skilled American workers by approximately $800–$1,500
  per year. He has concluded that "immigration redistributes
  wealth from those who compete with immigrants to those who
  use immigrants"—from working–class Americans to the wealthy
  and big business.[141]

- According to a 2018 Gallup survey, approximately 158 million people living outside America—almost half our current population—would immigrate to the United States if allowed.[142]

- The most recent statistics indicate that federal prisons house 26,678 criminal aliens, and that state and local jails and prisons house 169,300 criminal aliens. These numbers come even though the undocumented who commit crimes are 41% less likely to be incarcerated than native–born Americans who commit crimes.[143]

- By one estimate, illegal immigration poses net costs on American taxpayers—federal, state and, local—of approximately $116 billion every year.[144]

- During 2018, US border agents removed nearly 6,000 gang members in our country illegally.[145]

- By one account, nearly one in three women, and more than one in six men, report some form of sexual abuse on their journey to the border.[146]

- Each week, nearly 300 Americans die from heroin overdoses, with Mexico and our southern border the prime sources for the powerful narcotic.[147]

The Full Story

Legal immigration is one of the great sources of America's strength. Since before our nation's independence, the best and brightest people from all around the world have come to America to work hard for a better life. Our country continues to have one of the most generous immigration policies in the world, admitting more than one million legal permanent residents each year.[148]

But many of the people who come to America illegally, without going through the processes established by immigration law, pose a burden to American taxpayers.

The truth is that most people who come to America illegally will—over their lifetime—take more in public benefits than they will pay in taxes. Because these migrants drain the nation's resources on net, Americans, including legal immigrants, will have to work harder and pay more taxes to support this influx. And most future Americans will have a lower standard of living because of illegal immigration's burden.

Considering America's limited resources, growing debt, and underfunded priorities—such as infrastructure and our military—common sense suggests the federal government should attempt to discourage and stop illegal immigration. But for decades, politicians in Washington have done exactly the opposite. Federal policies have created irresistible benefits for those who come to America illegally. These benefits and incentives have created criminal enterprises that bring illegal workers to America, promote human trafficking, and smuggle illegal drugs and dangerous criminals from all over the world.

More importantly, encouraging illegal immigration unfairly harms legal immigrants. America already admits more legal permanent residents per year than any other nation in the world.[149] Legal immigrants have waited their turn, followed the rules, and worked hard to get here. If we allow certain people to skip the line—rewarding them for breaking the rules—we incentivize breaking rather than following the law, undermining respect for the rule of law that makes America attractive to immigrants in oppressed nations. It does a disservice both to legal immigrants and law-abiding citizens by encouraging lawlessness and organized crime at our borders, from gang and drug activity to human trafficking.

Birthright citizenship provides a perverse incentive for illegal immigration. This concept has encouraged women from other countries to immigrate (legally or illegally) during their pregnancy, so their child will automatically become a citizen at birth.

Once born a citizen, a child's parents can use the citizenship of that child (the so-called "anchor baby") to start chain migration, where parents can obtain visas and invite members of their extended family to immigrate to America. This loophole in our immigration laws helped create a wave of legal and illegal immigration after 1965. That year, Congress passed the Immigration and Nationality Act, eliminating the government's ability to selectively admit new citizens from countries of origin, and allowing the family sponsorship that promotes chain migration.[150]

Before 1965, many immigrants from Mexico and Central America came to America as temporary or seasonal workers. These immigrants often worked seasonally for several years, saved money, and opened their own businesses back in their home countries. This pattern benefited the immigrants themselves, their home countries, and Americans.

But the new law severely limited guest worker visas and permanent residents from south of our borders. The limits resulted in a dramatic rise in illegal immigration, which was magnified by new federal welfare, health care, and entitlement programs created in the 1960s. Illegal immigrants with children could access government benefits that gave them a higher standard of living than they could have ever dreamed of in their home country. As knowledge of America's rich government benefits spread throughout Mexico and Central America, many immigrants came to America not simply to work, but to work the system.

The change in America's immigration policy cut off the low-skilled, entry-level jobs that once represented the first step on the ladder of opportunity for many poor, young Americans. Americans suddenly had little motivation to take low-paying jobs, finding it easier and more profitable to take welfare benefits rather than compete with illegal immigrants.

Why They Lie

Progressive leaders know that if they open American borders to massive illegal immigration, and all the illegal immigrants today remain on welfare programs and win the right to vote, the Left will take control of the country. As a former Member of Congress, working closely with Democrat congressmen and senators for over 20 years, I have seen their ultimate goal of voting rights for illegal immigrants. When it comes to immigration policy, their goal is always amnesty, welfare, unionization, citizenship, and voting rights for over 10 million illegal immigrants, and as many additional illegal immigrants as can flow across America's borders. It has nothing to do with compassion or what is best for America. It has everything to do with the raw politics of power.

The Left now openly supports counting illegal immigrants as citizens in our census, creating many benefits for large, progressive states that encourage illegal immigration. The census count determines how much federal money flows to states for education, transportation, welfare, and many other federal programs. But more importantly, the census determines the allocation of congressional districts to states, and also helps to determine how many electoral college votes a state receives in presidential elections.[151]

By treating illegal immigrants as citizens, and abandoning centuries long efforts to assimilate them into our American culture and history while advocating for open borders, progressives diminish the importance of American citizenship in favor of global "citizenship." It's easier to radically change American politics to more authoritarian rule if you rapidly import new citizens from authoritarian countries and don't expect them to adopt American ideals, or even our common language! America should function as the great melting pot, where diverse peoples come together under common principles and shared national culture. As our national motto says, *E pluribus unum*—"Out of many, one."

Unions in America have also advocated for illegal immigration, which forces millions of undocumented workers to join unions and pay dues to get jobs. Of course, the union bosses always pretended to oppose illegal immigration to avoid offending their American members, but they continue to support the *status quo*. As key funders and leaders of progressive, leftist national coalitions, unions have played a large role in making sure the flow of illegal workers continues unabated.

The Trump Administration's insistence on stopping illegal immigration has angered many of the special interests who benefit from the practice. Though initially slow to respond to public pressure against illegal immigration, Republican leaders in Congress eventually shifted their position to make border control one of their top political priorities.

While legal immigration once created more opportunity, prosperity, and wealth for all Americans, it has become another way for other countries to prey on the hard work and success of the American people. Illegal immigration has compounded this problem by allowing illegal aliens to access public benefits, while sending American dollars back to their home countries.

Open borders are anything but compassionate. Unrestricted immigration with lucrative packages of public benefits not only hurt Americans, but often hurt immigrants—whether legal or illegal. Open borders lead to a flood of low-skilled workers that compete with low-income Americans for jobs, increase criminal and gang activity, and encourage deadly illegal drugs and weapons. Certainly, many good people come to America illegally, but we must control our borders to keep our citizens and legal immigrants safe, secure, and prosperous. We cannot remain a beacon of freedom and hope to the world if we trample our own rule of law, and encourage the world's criminals and terrorists to walk across our borders unimpeded. A country without borders is no country at all.

BIG LIE #9:
IF YOU DON'T AGREE WITH THE LEFT, THEN YOU ARE A RACIST

*"If you have a problem figuring out whether
you're for me or [Donald] Trump,
then you ain't black!"*
— Vice President Joe Biden[152]

*"[Trump] has amassed power through racist appeals.
He's held onto it by holding onto the worst impulses of
American character: nativism, racism, extremism, isolationism.
All the things in that have held us back in the past."*
— Jon Meacham, presidential historian[153]

"White people, you are the problem."
— Dahleen Glanton, Chicago Tribune columnist[154]

The Lie:

If you hold conservative political views, you are a racist.

The Facts:

- In 2018, the poverty rate of African American families with children and two married parents stood at 8.3%. The poverty rate of African American single–parent families stood several times higher—27.2% in the case of children raised by a male head–of–household, and 37.8% in the case of children raised by a female head–of–household.[155]

- The 2017 Tax Cuts and Jobs Act created opportunity zones, providing tax breaks for individuals and companies that invest in low–income areas. Leftists in Congress like Reps. Alexandria Ocasio Cortez (D–NY) and Rashida Tlaib (D–MI) have proposed getting rid of these job–creating zones rather than reforming and improving the program.[156]

- In the nation's capital, over 82% of Washington, D.C. opportunity scholarship recipients identify as African American, with a further 12% identifying as Latino. Yet leftist politicians want to outlaw this important school choice program.[157]

- African Americans represent 38% of the nation's abortions—a percentage nearly three times the African American share of the population (13%).[158]

The Full Story

Do you sometimes wonder, just who are "they"….and, conversely, who are "we?"

For purposes of analyzing the lies that "we" are fed on a daily basis, I consider that "we" are conservatives, whether voters, political leaders, or activists. We are people committed to our faith, and regularly attend church or synagogues. We believe in marriage and the nuclear family, in the special roles both mothers and fathers play in development of children. We love America, and celebrate our nation's history. We own guns, go hunting and protect our families, support law enforcement, and believe in the rule of law, property rights, and respect for the rights of others.

We believe that our brilliant and prescient Framers gave us the building blocks of the greatest country the world has ever known, one that is truly exceptional, which has served as a beacon of light to millions over the centuries of America's existence. We are hardworking, we pay taxes, we take care of our children, we are blue collar and white collar and no collar at all. We believe in the

Constitution, including its guarantees of our rights to worship, to pray, to speak, to be heard, to bear arms, and to live in a society where the people are sovereign and the government limited.

We are the small business owners who open in the morning and close up at night, and who are not looking for a handout, but certainly wish the government wouldn't make it quite so attractive for people not to work, so that we can fill the jobs in our stores and our businesses. We believe in the sanctity of life for every race and religion, and we believe that we are all precious in God's eyes. That's who "we" are.

They? They are the "smart people"—the leftist politicians, activists, academics, and pundits who look with disdain at those of us who pray, hunt, or respect the flag. They are Hollywood, journalists on the coasts, corporate elites, and LGBTQ+ activists who scorn us for "rejecting science," and then tell us there are fifty–eight genders. They are socialists, Marxists, collectivists, who don't believe in free enterprise, and who believe that with enough government dominance over its citizens, humans can literally control the climate....to stop it from changing. They are the founders of multi–million dollar rip–off entities like Black Lives Matter, the Southern Policy Law Center, the Human Rights Campaign, the ACLU, and on and on. They are the builders of the networks and organizations to "transform" America into their image ... which bears no resemblance to the America that "we" love.

And if you do not agree with their vision for America? Well, that makes you a racist. And "they" can tell if you are a racist by the things you believe.

Our society today is full of studies, articles, media reports, books, and speakers who are lecturing us that our conservative beliefs make us racist.

Just this year, the National Museum of African American History and Culture—part of the taxpayer-financed Smithsonian Institution in Washington, D.C.—released a new online project called "Talking About White Culture in the United States." The site featured an infographic that used a consultant's work from 1990 to list the "Aspects and Assumptions of Whiteness and White Culture."[159] These racist "white" characteristics included:

- "Rugged Individualism: self-reliance"
- "Nuclear family...husband is breadwinner...wife is homemaker"
- "Children should have own rooms, be independent"
- "Emphasis on scientific method: Objective, rational thinking"
- "Primacy of western (Greek, Roman) and Judeo-Christian tradition"
- "Protestant Work Ethic: Hard work is key to success, work before play"
- "No tolerance for deviation from single god concept"
- "Respect authority"
- "Plan for future...delayed gratification...tomorrow will be better"
- "Justice: Based on English common law...protect property"
- "Be polite"

Yes—according to this chart, we are all racists for being polite, respecting authority, and believing in common wisdom passed down from our grandparents. Apparently, teaching children to love God, to be self-reliant, and to plan for the future is only something racist white people do.

After a backlash, the African American History Museum removed the graphic from its site, admitting that the "chart [did] not contribute to the productive discussion we had intended."[160] But the move didn't answer a basic underlying question: Why did anyone believe that concepts like self-reliance and science were racist to begin with? You don't know whether to laugh or to cry at the sheer madness of it all. It's actual racism disguised as a theory to combat racism.

Yet this is the type of backwards thinking that for decades has permeated our colleges and universities—the places we send our children and pay hundreds of thousands of dollars to teach this nonsense. These are the messages that Hollywood has been slipping into movies for decades—and we keep trying to ignore it all. But we can't ignore it any longer.

The Left has confused too many Americans with their lies, and it's time we set the record straight.

Let's look at just a few key issues facing our country today...that "they" oppose....but which "we" support. And then let's talk about who is racist.

School Choice: The Secretary of Education, Betsy DeVos, has dedicated her life to educational opportunities for all children. Under her leadership, the Trump Administration has consistently advanced school choice opportunities, so that children in low-income families are not trapped in failing schools. According to a survey of likely 2020 voters, Democrats for Education Reform (DFER) found that 81% of voters—including 81% of Democratic primary voters and 89% of black Democratic primary voters—support expanding "access to more choices and options within the public school system, including magnet schools, career academies, and public charter schools."[161] Black inner city parents desperately want their children to have the same choices in schools that wealthier suburban parents have. It is the teachers' unions and liberal elites who keep those barriers from falling, trapping minority children in failing government schools.

Pro Life: Progressive liberals support Planned Parenthood, founded by notorious eugenicist Margaret Sanger. Sanger promoted birth control in order to advance a controversial "Negro Project," and wrote in her autobiography about an approach to "breeding" for "the gradual suppression, elimination, and eventual extinction, of defective stocks—those human weeds which threaten the blooming of the finest flowers of American civilization."[162]

Sanger's legacy lives on in the high abortion rates of African American babies. For instance, in New York City, even after a nearly 30% reduction in the African American abortion rate from 2013 to 2017, almost as many black babies were aborted (20,569) than were born (21,992) in 2017.[163]

Tax Cuts, Regulatory Reform and Economic Opportunity: "They" would have us believe that only by supporting big government programs can you demonstrate your anti-racist credentials. But the reality is the opposite. Since the Great Society programs of the 1960s, the US government has spent trillions of dollars in anti-poverty and "helping" programs—over $22 trillion, by one count—yet the poverty rate has barely declined since the mid-1960s.[164]

Do the liberal elites praise the great progress resulting from all those federal programs? Quite the opposite. They continue to bray about the horrible, dark nature of America. On the other hand, thanks to the economic programs of the Trump Administration, with the Tax Cuts and Jobs Act of 2017, deregulation, and other pro-growth policies, the African-American unemployment rate reached the historically low rate of 5.4% in October 2019.[165] In other words, it is *conservative* policies that lift minorities out of poverty by creating jobs and economic opportunity.

Criminal Justice Reform: In June 2018, President Trump commuted the sentence of a non-violent drug offender, Alice Marie Johnson, who had been in prison for more than twenty years. Around the same time, the Trump White House pushed

Congress to significantly reform the criminal justice system, to ease sentences for nonviolent crimes. The First Step Act, signed into law by President Trump in December 2018, gives judges greater latitude in imposing mandatory minimum sentences, allows inmates to earn increased good conduct time, increases programming to address inmates' needs, offers earned time credits for completion of training programs and/or productive activities, and expands opportunities for inmate placement into residential re–entry centers or home confinement.[166]

One would think that "they" would support and applaud this effort on the part of the Trump Administration. But when Alice Marie Johnson spoke to the Republican National Convention, lauding the efforts of the Trump Administration on criminal justice reform and thanking the President for commuting her sentence so she could be reunited with her family after twenty years, *Politico* called her a "prop."[167] Ms. Johnson's response was swift and strong. "What amazes me about the things that are being said is that another former prisoner spoke at the [Democratic National Convention] last week, and she was not called a prop for choosing to speak there, yet I don't have the choice to speak where I want to," Johnson said during an interview. "I'm not a prop, and I'm not a puppet. I make my own choices as to what I'd like to do."[168]

Marriage and the Nuclear Family: Black Lives Matter has as one of its central tenets the destruction of the nuclear family: "We disrupt the western–prescribed nuclear family structure requirement."[169] The left–wing Southern Poverty Law Center has declared Christian organizations that believe in the nuclear family and support traditional marriage as "hate groups."[170] SPLC disguises its hostility toward Christian organizations behind a veil of supporting the LGBTQ+ agenda. But make no mistake: In the Left's eyes, if you believe in Christian principles, you are a member of a hate group—and a racist.

The evidence proves that the best way to lift black families—indeed, lift all families—from poverty is *marriage*. But these left-wing so-called anti-racist organizations want to undermine our most proven anti-poverty solution.

These are just a few conservative policies and principles that actually contribute to the progress and success of black Americans. But if we believe in these principles that actually work, and do not toe the line on liberal, progressive issues and candidates, then we are racists. Never mind that the facts demonstrate the opposite. And never forget that any minorities who join with conservatives in supporting conservative policies and principles must be puppets or props. It is outrageous.

Why is it so important for the Left to twist the facts to convince everyone (including us) that "we" and others who believe as we do are racist? Why is that an essential goal of the post-modern leftist elites?

Conservative intellectual and author Roger Kimball argues that "it is worth stepping back to ask what is it about the term 'racism' that silences conversation and sends an anticipatory shudder of delight down the spines of politically correct vigilantes of virtue. Like the word 'heretic' in an earlier age, 'racism' is more weapon than word. Its primary effect is not to describe but to intimidate, ostracize, and silence."[171]

More weapon than word. Indeed.

And what is the goal? It intends to ensure that, even when black voters share our views on public policy proposals and issues, they will continue to choose Democratic candidates over Republicans.

Today, the black community is underserved in American politics for two reasons: Democrats know they don't have to do anything to keep the votes of black Americans. All they have to do is convince them that Republicans are racist. And Republicans know that no matter what they do, black voters will never support GOP candidates.

So both parties talk a lot, and nothing changes.

I served in the House and Senate as a Republican, but I have been as critical of Republicans as Democrats. Republican leaders in Washington rarely take strong stands for the things they say they believe. And too often, they are as much a part of the Washington Swamp as the Democrats. My point is, I'm not blind to the failures of the Republicans. I've spent my whole career pointing them out! But compared to the Democrats, Republicans are angels.

In 1857, the Supreme Court—controlled by Democrat justices— issued a ruling, *Dred Scott v. Sandford*, which said slaves were not citizens of the United States, but the legal property of their owners.[172] The court in this decision also prohibited the federal government from eliminating slavery in any state. The Democrat party announced they would abide by this decision in their party platform for the 1860 presidential election.

After the Civil War, Democrats worked against equal rights for black Americans. Most freed slaves became Republicans, and many ran for public office. But after losing the war and the presidency, southern Democrats came to rely on the Ku Klux Klan as *a de facto* militia, using violence to intimidate black people and promote white supremacy.[173]

Democrats continued to control most southern states for decades after the Civil War, enacting Jim Crow laws that denied voting and citizenship rights to blacks, ensuring generations of segregation. The Republican Party supported integration, but found itself a small minority political party in the segregated South. It was the Democrats who blocked black children from attending white schools, forced black passengers to sit in the back of buses, and fought to protect segregation.

In 1896, the Supreme Court ruling in *Plessy vs. Ferguson* permitted "separate but equal" treatment by race.[174] This decision allowed governments and businesses—in the case of Plessy, railroads—to segregate blacks from whites. This 7 to 1 ruling reflected the Jim Crow Laws enacted by Democrats in the South after the Civil War, and maintained state–sponsored segregation and discrimination until the 1960s.

Interestingly, in the Plessy case, the one dissenting vote on the high court came from Justice John Marshall Harlan. Originally a Democrat and a Kentucky slave owner, Harlan initially opposed the Emancipation Proclamation. But after the Civil War, when Harlan saw the injustices and violence the Democrats were using against blacks, he became a Republican and a strong advocate for civil rights.

Democrats and segregation ruled the American South until the 1960s. In 1957, Republicans helped to pass the first federal civil rights legislation since Reconstruction; in the Senate, all 18 of the votes against the legislation came from Democrats.[175]

In 1963, President Kennedy proposed another new civil rights bill to end segregation in public places, among other important reforms. The House passed the legislation, but Democrat opposition in the Senate killed the bill. After Kennedy's assassination, President Lyndon Johnson sent the legislation back to Congress. The House again passed the bill, but Democrats in the Senate led a 54–day filibuster to thwart the bill's passage. However, Republicans finally overcame the Democrat filibuster, and the bill passed. In the votes on final passage in the House and Senate, a larger percentage of Republicans voted for the Civil Rights Act of 1964 (80%) than Democrats (64%).[176] Yet the myth persists within the black community that Democrats have historically advocated for their interests.

President Johnson also initiated his "War on Poverty" that included new welfare and public assistance programs that shifted black votes from Republicans to Democrats. Even though these programs helped to destroy the black family structure and trap millions of black families in intergenerational poverty, black Americans are instructed by the media that *Republicans* are their enemies and *Democrats* their friends.[177]

Are some conservatives racist? Regrettably, despite all the progress we've made as a nation, I'm sure there are some racists on both sides of the aisle. But after twenty years in politics—whether in Washington D.C., or my hometown of Greenville, South Carolina—I haven't met a person who discriminated against someone because of the color of his skin.

Why They Lie

Race is the strategy and security blanket of the Left. If racism became ineffective as the magic sword against conservatives, the progressives would lose their bogeyman. For decades, the Democratic Party has been allowed to ignore their party's racist history and have presented themselves as black Americans' only defenders.

So the leftists in America, elite media, Hollywood, the universities, the public employee unions, and Democratic politicians shriek racism where it doesn't exist to distract voters both black AND white from the high cost of left–wing policy failures and the damage done to generations of black Americans from those policies.

One only need look at every major city in America to see the empirical evidence of the failure of liberal social policy and the progressive agenda.

The "smart people" refuse to accept that what is tearing at the fabric of black America are the liberal big government policies that have decimated black families and neighborhoods, the corrupt big city politicians, and the contemptuous attitudes leveled at any minority person who dares to step outside the prescribed sphere of what a black person is "supposed" to think or espouse.

Generations of disadvantage and discrimination take a long time to overcome. But we will never eliminate the residual impact of historical racism by perpetuating the myth that massive numbers of our fellow Americans are bigots.

"We" are not racist. The Republican Party is the party of Abraham Lincoln, which came into existence during the fight to end slavery. America's problems today are not the result of systemic, institutional racism. America still has flaws, but it remains a land of opportunity and a shining light to people everywhere.

Solving problems requires an understanding of their real causes. If we want to blame all of our nation's problems on racism, we are lying to ourselves and we'll never solve any of them.

And we cannot reduce racism in America by spreading crackpot theories that promote division, fear, and hatred for people because of the color of their skin, or because people embrace timeless values and principles that made our nation great.

As Martin Luther King, Jr. said: "Love is the only force capable of transforming an enemy into friend."

LIE #10:
THE CONSTITUTION
IS OUTDATED, UNFAIR,
AND UNNECESSARY

"Documents or texts written 2,000 years ago or 200 years ago should not control our ability to advance the human race and do what needs to be done in the 21st century to create a more enlightened community based in justice and compassion for all."
— Matthew Dowd[178]

"The United States Constitution is terse and old, and it guarantees relatively few rights."
— Adam Litpak, The New York Times[179]

"I would not look to the United States Constitution if I were drafting a constitution"
— Justice Ruth Bader Ginsburg[180]

The Lie:

The United States Constitution is an outdated document that stands in the way of progress and only benefits a select few.

The Facts:

• The U.S. Constitution is the most successful and widely copied national political charter in the history of western civilization. At the time of its bicentennial, 160 of 170 countries had modeled their governing documents on the written Constitution our Framers signed in September 1787.[181]

- The U.S. Constitution splits federal power: A bicameral Congress writes laws; the president executes them; and the judiciary ensures their constitutionality. Dividing authority among minimally overlapping branches makes our system of government simple in form yet complex in its underlying theory.[182]

- The Bill of Rights doesn't grant rights to the people—it restricts government from infringing on basic God–given human rights that have become the standard of civilized countries around the world. These include freedom of religion, speech, assembly, press, and the rights to bear arms and to petition government.

- Over more than two centuries of its history, the Constitution has adapted to fit the concept of a "more perfect union," extending the blessings of liberty to more Americans.

- Of the 27 amendments to the Constitution, two–thirds (18) of them have expanded Americans' rights and liberties. Eleven (the Bill of Rights and the 14th Amendment) protect Americans from government abuses and give them due process rights; six (15th, 17th, 19th, 23rd, 24th, and 26th Amendments) expanded the franchise; and the 13th Amendment abolished slavery.

- Article V set a high bar for amending the Constitution: A 2/3rds majority of each house of Congress, plus ratification by 3/4ths of states. The process requires a broad national consensus in favor of a position before amending our nation's founding document, creating stability and avoiding chaos.

The Full Story

Progressives hate the United States Constitution.

Why? It's old. It was written by a bunch of straight white men. It has fixed standards. It divides and decentralizes power. It makes it hard to control everything. It forces the Left to debate and compromise with people who disagree with them. In short, the Constitution poses an obstacle to the Left's plan to centralize political, economic, and cultural power—which means the Constitution works!

The Constitution exists to serve all Americans equally. While the angry Left resents that, everyone else should be grateful for it. We are all in the minority sometimes, and it's good to have our rights laid out in writing to keep power–hungry people from taking them away.

America's objectives and rules were established by our two founding documents: the Declaration of Independence and the Constitution. The Declaration provides the reasons for America's existence (equality, liberty, the protection of rights and justice) and reminds us that a just government must serve with the consent of the people.

The goals of equality and justice set forth in the Declaration and Constitution did not become reality the day these documents were signed. Instead, they became high standards challenging generations of Americans to work to achieve. And that's what has happened. We have not betrayed these aspirations; we have pursued them. America continues to move toward the aspirational goals set forward by our founding documents.

The Constitution established the "rule of law" as the operational philosophy for our new country. The Framers of our founding document believed strongly in the rule of law and adamantly opposed the "rule of men."

Our Framers painfully remembered how King George III of England, their former master, operated totally by the "rule of men"—one man, actually. The King did not grant the American colonists the rights of English citizens required by law. King George had the power to make arbitrary decisions and enforce them with no accountability. The rules didn't matter.

The Constitution is not conservative, liberal, or progressive. It provides a set of rules for government, and rights for citizens established in advance so Americans can know the rules of the game. It assures Americans that their government has limited powers and they have guaranteed freedoms. Under the Constitution, all citizens can live in freedom if they and the government follow the rules. Ironically, citizens can only have freedom if they voluntarily follow the rules that protect the rights of others.

Progressives don't want a set of rules they have to follow when they are in power. They eschew any moorings, traditions, or fixed set of rules established by others. They do not want any limits on what *they* can do—just limits on *you*.

Would it make more sense to throw out the Constitution and let Congress make all the decisions? Or, better yet, why not let everyone who lives in America vote on the big issues? Today, with the internet and instant communications, we don't need a Congress to decide what we should do. We could all vote on everything from our homes. Let the majority rule. Isn't that how democracy works?

That's exactly how democracy works, and it is exactly why the Framers did not create a democracy. They created a republic, with elected representatives from all the states who would vote for the collective good of all the people—not individual or special interests. America's Framers knew that a pure democracy would create a "majority rules" system, where the mob would call the shots. In fact, Article IV, Section 4 of the Constitution says that "the United States shall guarantee to every State in the Union a Republican Form of Government"—*not* a democracy.

When the majority rules absolutely, minorities lose absolutely. The vastly wealthy leftist network wants the "majority" to rule in America because—with control of education, the news media, the entertainment industry, big corporations, and millions of government workers—they believe they can control public opinion. With 51% of the voters, they can control everything in America.

Do we really want 51% of Americans to force their views on the other 49% – to tell them what to believe, what they can say, what their children learn in school, who will be their doctor and what medical treatments they can receive, where they will work, what products will be produced, what the media can and can't report, what will be allowed on the internet, and how they will vote?

We have majority–rule "democracies" in Russia, Venezuela, and in other countries around the world. Somehow, the ruling elite always get re–elected—and get very rich too. And somehow, the poor and ethnic minorities always get poorer and more neglected.

Today, if Americans had their way, they would change how we elect our president. A slender majority of Americans now support amending the Constitution to eliminate the Electoral College and elect our presidents with a national popular vote—that is, the candidate who receives the most votes nationwide would become our president.[183] Why is that a bad idea? Because nine or fewer of America's largest states could decide our presidential elections.

America's Framers created the Electoral College to prevent a few heavily populated, large states from deciding our presidential elections. Remember, the Framers focused on maintaining the independence and autonomy of individual states. They did not want an all–powerful national government with an aristocracy of elites, or a pure democracy. They wanted a hybrid system that took the best parts of all forms of government and avoided the worst parts.

So the Constitution created a Congress, a presidency, and a Supreme Court. It gave the national government some powers, and state governments all the rest.

The Constitution gives each state the same number of delegates to the Electoral College as their number of congressional representatives—a combination of the number of congressmen and senators from each state. So while heavily populated states still have an advantage, every state has at least three delegates to the Electoral College.

But the Constitution doesn't keep us from changing. It established an amendment process that allows a supermajority of the states to change it in any way they like. If Americans come to a broad agreement that our founding document needs changing, the Constitution gives us the power to do it. But until we reach that consensus for change, the Constitution provides the foundation and framework for law and order—and for freedom.

OK, but isn't the Constitution elitist? Wasn't it written by a bunch of rich white men? Nope. The Framers of the Constitution included manufacturers, physicians, small farmers, and a minister; several, like Ben Franklin and Alexander Hamilton, rose from poverty and humble origins.[184] Others were prominent citizens from the states, but not necessarily wealthy. And if they had been elitist, they would not have signed a Constitution that limited their power. They would not have put political power in the hands of the common people.

Throughout history, there has never been another group of national leaders who came together to give away their power. Tyrants always say they are acting on behalf of the people, but it never turns out that way. America is different—it has been from the beginning.

One of the most amazing things about the Constitution is that the Framers knew their limits. They recognized that they didn't have all the answers and that none of them, being human, could be trusted to have total control over others.

So they created a system of checks and balances that allowed for changing leaders and laws over time without chaos. They established regular elections to keep government in line with the will of the people, and three co-equal branches with different roles that guard against each other accumulating tyrannical power. Congress creates the laws. The President carries out the law. The judiciary enforces penalties and judges new laws against the rights enshrined in the Constitution. As James Madison wrote in *Federalist No. 51*, "ambition must be made to counteract ambition." By setting up three branches of government as equal guardians of authority, the Constitution did just that.

In the last few decades, however, civics education has been chucked from school curricula, or replaced by progressive propaganda about the "dead white male" Framers' unfair and outdated Constitutional model of government.[185]

It sounds crazy when you think about it for a moment. The United States is the world's oldest republic.[186] The Constitution, as amended over the last two centuries, has allowed Americans to build the world's freest, fairest, safest, most prosperous, and most stable nation in the history of the world. And yet a recent survey found that 70% of self-described liberals and 79% of self-described "very liberal" respondents supported the creation of "a new American constitution that better reflects our diversity as a people."[187]

Here the Left gives away their real intentions. Diversity? Are you kidding me!? The modern Left *hates* the most important diversity of all: diversity of thought. They claim to embrace peoples of all races, genders, cultures, and faiths—but ONLY if you agree with their politically correct agenda.

The Left doesn't tolerate diversity. They want people to think exactly alike—otherwise they sic social media outrage mobs after them to get them fired, demonetized, or "de-platformed." Look at progressives' unrepeatable comments about black conservatives like Sen. Tim Scott (R–SC) or Housing and Urban Development Secretary Ben Carson.

The progressive paradigm is essentially defined by its *intolerance* —its insistence that anyone disagreeing with them must do so for hateful, sexist, bigoted, transphobic, or racist reasons. The old Left would call dissent the highest form of patriotism. The new progressive, totalitarian Left thinks dissent from their policy agenda not just wrong, but evil. And when someone is evil, they don't have to be argued with, they are to be censored, shut out from society, and denounced.

And those "approved" progressive thoughts and policies are ever changing. Twenty years ago, most Democrats supported deporting illegal immigrants and building a border wall. Now, that's considered racist. Until he ran for re-election as President in 2012, Barack Obama opposed gay marriage. He would be decried as a bigot today. Lifelong feminists like *Harry Potter* creator J.K. Rowling have been vilified by the Left for daring to say transgender men are not biological women. And lifelong gay rights activist Andrew Sullivan has been forced out of work at liberal media because he spoke out against the ridiculousness of critical race theory.[188]

That's why liberal progressives hate the Constitution—because it was written for a diverse and tolerant nation. Indeed, the United States was the most diverse nation in the world before it even united into a nation. New England Puritans, Pennsylvania Quakers, and Appalachian Presbyterians shared superficial similarities, but they certainly didn't see themselves as having much in common. Neither did city slickers in Boston and New York think they had many overlapping interests with farmers and backwoodsmen on the frontiers. The American colonies held Christians of every denomination, Jews, Deists, immigrants from all over the world. Part of the reason the colonies needed a new form of government was that they *were* so different.

The Constitution's genius lay in harnessing the vast differences of the American people to the benefit everyone. The Framers separated governmental powers, so that different people would make, enforce, and interpret the law. They established different tiers of government, so that the national central government would have powers that were specified and few, while the various (*diverse!*) states would retain the bulk of governing authority.

The Constitution protects the American people from centralized authoritarianism—whether it comes from the political right or the Left, from insiders or outsiders, from the rich oligarchs or poor revolutionaries.

Under our Constitution, America's diversity of states – red and blue, richer and poorer, urban and rural – became a strength, not a weakness. Americans could be united because they were allowed to be different. That's exactly why we need the Constitution now, more than ever.

The Constitution is not outdated; in fact, it perfectly suits our era of deep political division and conspicuous national diversity. There is nothing inherently wrong with political disagreement. Any nation of 330 million will of course have many differences. But there is no threat to the republic if we allow Vermonters and Texans to be different. And there is no threat to any other state if we let these states govern themselves differently. This pluralist mentality perfectly fits our nation's motto: *E pluribus unum*—"Out of many, one."

But today, many people in politics skip over the Constitution's call for consensus and instead try to decide every political issue as a nationwide, zero–sum fight to the death, where the other side is evil and compromise impossible. The Left doesn't want to compromise, but they know they can't win enough elections to ram through their unpopular agenda. So instead they blame the Constitution for obstructing "progress."

Why They Lie

What civics curricula don't teach and what leftist politicians won't admit is that constitutional government makes life better for the American people, but worse for the politicians themselves. Under the Constitution, Congress serves as the pre-eminent branch of the federal government—passing laws, overseeing the Administration, adjusting the budget according to performance, updating and reforming old policies, and hammering out compromises between competing interests, regions, and parties. Doing that, though, leaves a long paper trail of how representatives vote. The American people could see exactly what senators and representatives voted for and against—and that kind of responsibility and transparency would make their re-election campaigns tougher. So they just don't bother.

Most politicians don't bother, but not because they have tried the Constitution and found it unworkable. Instead, lawmakers today have found legislating according to the Constitution to be hard work, and think it easier to do nothing with lots of bluster.

The Constitution is not the cause of Washington dysfunction. The Constitution is the solution to it.

If you think I, a conservative, am defending the Constitution because it sets conservative policies, you haven't read it. The Constitution doesn't set policy at all. There's nothing in there about tax rates or budget priorities or whether China is a friend or a foe. The Constitution just sets fixed rules for how policy gets made in the first place. This may seem like a small detail, but it is the core of every freedom we take for granted. Under the Constitution, the federal government cannot just do whatever it wants – to us or for us. It must follow specific rules, which establish clear lines of accountability between the people, the politicians, and the policies.

The Left wants you to believe the Constitution is outdated, unfair and unnecessary, because they want to impose laws by any means necessary. If they can't win a vote in Congress, they want judges to legislate from the bench, or the President to create new laws by executive fiat.

The truth is: The Constitution is everything the Left isn't.
The Constitution treats everyone equally—regardless of race, creed, color, or politics. The Left believes progressives should rule, and everyone else should obey.

The Constitution requires transparent, accountable policymaking where the government works for the people. Progressives believe the people should work for the government.

The Constitution seeks compromise and consensus. Progressives want to slander and steamroll all opposition to their ideological goals.

The Constitution tolerates diversity by allowing different states to make different laws according to their different values. The Left wants you to consider all values besides their own evil, and laws based on alternative values illegitimate.

The Constitution is forever young, forever flexible, and open to every new generation of policy reforms and proposals. No matter how big or how diverse American becomes, the Constitution can protect all Americans' equal rights.

America's Constitution created a foundation for equality, freedom, and prosperity that has lasted for many generations, and nurtured the greatest nation in the history of the world. Let's not throw it away based on a bunch of lies.

Conclusion: The Sum of All Lies

The Bible says, "if you know the truth, the truth will set you free." The opposite is true with lies. Believing lies traps you, imprisons you, subjugates you to the liars. As Ronald Reagan said in his famous 1964 speech "A Time for Choosing," "It isn't so much that liberals are ignorant; it's just that they know so much that isn't so."

There was a time when leftists could at least suggest their ideas in good faith, in a spirit of curiosity and experimentation. But countries all over the world have tried various forms of modern progressivism for a century now—socialism, communism, fascism, national socialism, social democracy, and now, various strands of "wokeness" and weaponized political correctness. These efforts have led to conformity, stagnancy, fear, rigidity, division, dysfunction, and weakness. As a system of philosophy and a system of politics, progressive leftism just doesn't work.

As a system of propaganda, however, of fantasy world–building and moral bullying, it works just as well as it did under every oppressive regime in history. But progressivism increasingly appears exhausted as a movement of political reform, having morphed into a moralizing marketing scheme for the American elite's corporate religion.

Progressivism has always been obsessed with power. It focuses on persuading ordinary Americans to give *their* power to elites who are already some of the most powerful people in the world—so that they can wield it instead. These same elites already run our entertainment and news media; they run our education system; they exert overwhelming control over our culture and politics; and they have almost total control of most of America's largest industries, especially the biggest technology firms. They use that power to lie to you, manipulate and control you—to mold your worldview so that no matter what new information or experience comes in, you have the same reaction: to give them *more* of your power.

That's why they tell you God doesn't exist. They know if you believe in God and try to follow His truth, you would start to distrust the selfishness, materialism, and dishonesty of our elites. You might start wondering whether such people really ought to have so much power over your life. They know if you trust in God, you won't need to trust in them.

They tell you America is a racist nation, born in hate and white supremacy, not because it's true, but to shame you. If you think America is garbage, you're more likely to support their greedy efforts to seize total control so they can reshape it in their image.

They tell you the Earth's climate is in crisis, and surround you with frightening warnings and threats about what will happen if you don't surrender your power to them. They know that the science works against them, so they bully and threaten anyone who questions their orthodoxy.

They tell you that white people and men enjoy oppressive privileges to distract you from the fact that the political, cultural, and economic experiments progressives have run for decades have failed. "Don't look at the schools, government programs, moral values, and institutions we have monopoly control over! It's not our fault! It's the evil straight white men!"

They tell you that capitalism helps the rich and hurts everyone else, to trick you into letting them create more of the socialist policies that have turned government insiders into billionaires, while burdening ordinary citizens with limited opportunities and trillions in debt.

They tell you big government will help the poor, despite decades of big government doing the exact opposite—destroying families, killing jobs, shattering communities, and failing the poor, the sick, and the vulnerable.

They tell you borders are racist, not because it is true or because all countries should be borderless. They clamor for open borders so poor immigrants will help rich people keep low–skilled wages low and vote for Democrat candidates. Anti–racism has nothing to do with it.

None of this is about justice, racial equality, or any other political virtue. It is about fear: agree with us, the elites say, or pay the price. Disagree, and we'll send the social media mobs after you, call you a bigot and a misogynist, and get you fired or shut down your business. Be woke or be canceled—as *The Godfather* might say, it's the offer you can't refuse.

Yet for all their power over our culture, our schools, and our politics, most Americans still do resist, at least privately. Most Americans still love their country and their freedom. They distrust elites selling them a warped view of the world that seems only to give *them* more power. For all the cultural power of the progressive Left, most Americans can still see through a lie.

And that terrifies them.

We've shown how easy it is to refute some of the biggest lies being used to destroy the principles and practices that have made America the greatest country in history and made life better for billions of people. But nobody can stop the lies forever. The lying will continue.

We all need to take control of the lenses that shape how we think. We need to build our own narratives based on facts—real truth. If "your truth" is based on a popular narrative instead of facts, you have been set up by others as a useful idiot. That's what the elites—the media, the academics, the CEOs, the big tech firms, and the politicians—want: to keep you passive, ignorant, and pliable.

That's no way to live. Be brave. Go out and find the truth.

Speak the truth. Live the truth.

True citizenship means doing the work of creating *your own worldview*, not just borrowing someone else's.

That's what America has always been about: giving everyone the freedom to chart their own course, try and fail, learn and succeed, until we figure out what works best for us.

The Left wants you to trust them—but I hope that you will seek the truth and trust yourself instead.

Footnotes

[1] Quoted in Ed Pilkington, "Obama Angers Midwest Voters with Guns and Religion Remark," The Guardian April 14, 2008, https://www.theguardian.com/world/2008/apr/14/barackobama.uselections2008.

[2] Quoted in Gary Younge, "The Capped Crusader," The Guardian October 4, 2003, https://www.theguardian.com/film/2003/oct/04/michaelmoore.features.

[3] David Briggs, "No Time for Crime: Study Finds More Religious Communities Have Lower Rates of Black, White, and Latino Violence," Huffington Post February 3, 2014, https://www.huffpost.com/entry/no-time-for-crime-study-f_b_4384046.

[4] Kanita Dervic, et al., "Religious Affiliation and Suicide Attempt," American Journal of Psychiatry 161:12 (December 2004), https://ajp.psychiatryonline.org/doi/full/10.1176/appi.ajp.161.12.2303.

[5] Shanshan Li, Laura Kubzansky, and Tyler VanderWeele, "Religious Service Attendance, Divorce, and Remarriage Among U.S. Nurses in Mid and Late Life," PLoS ONE 13:12 (December 3, 2018), https://www.ncbi.nlm.nih.gov/pmc/articles/PMC6277070/.

[6] "New Report Finds Religious People Are More Likely to Donate," Philanthropy Today October 25, 2017, https://www.philanthropydaily.com/religious-philanthropy-faith/.

[7] Karl Zinsmeister, "Less God, Less Giving," Philanthropy Winter 2019, https://www.philanthropyroundtable.org/philanthropy-magazine/less-god-less-giving.

[8] Ibid.

[9] Ibid.

[10] Amelia Thomson-DeVeaux and Daniel Cox, "The Christian Right Is Helping Drive Liberals Away from Religion," FiveThirtyEight September 18, 2019, https://fivethirtyeight.com/features/the-christian-right-is-helping-drive-liberals-away-from-religion/.

[11] Fox News, "Bill Barr: Antifa Is 'New Form of Guerrilla Urban Warfare,'" August 9, 2020, https://www.foxnews.com/transcript/bill-barr-antifa-is-new-form-of-urban-guerrilla-warfare.

[12] Carol Glatz, "On 50th Anniversary of Earth Day, Pope Francis Calls for 'Ecological Conversion,'" Catholic News Service April 22, 2020, https://www.americamagazine.org/faith/2020/04/22/50th-anniversary-earth-day-pope-francis-calls-ecological-conversion.

[13] Holmes Lybrand and Tara Subramaniam, "Fact Check: Beto O'Rourke Said He Would Support Removing Tax Exemptions for Religious Institutions That Oppose Same Sex Marriage. Is that Legal?" CNN October 11, 2019, https://www.cnn.com/2019/10/11/politics/beto-orourke-lgbtq-gay-marriage-church-fact-check/index.html.

[14] Matthew Brown, "Fact Check: Did Kentucky Order Police to Record the License Plates of Easter Churchgoers?" USA Today April 13, 2020, https://www.usatoday.com/story/news/factcheck/2020/04/13/coronavirus-fact-check-ky-police-recorded-info-easter-churchgoers/2980574001/.

[15] Elizabeth Bartholet, "Homeschooling: Parent Rights Absolutism vs. Child Rights to Education and Protection," Arizona Law Review 62:1 (2020), https://arizonalawreview.org/pdf/62-1/62arizlrev1.pdf.

[16] Quoted in Erin O'Donnell, "The Risks of Homeschooling," Harvard Magazine May-June 2020, https://harvardmagazine.com/2020/05/right-now-risks-homeschooling.

[17] Quoted in David Paul Kuhn and Ben Smith, "Messianic Rhetoric Infuses Obama Rallies," Politico December 9, 2007, https://www.politico.com/story/2007/12/messianic-rhetoric-infuses-obama-rallies-007281.

[18] CNN, "President: National Exit Poll," November 4, 2008, https://www.cnn.com/ELECTION/2008/results/polls/#val=USP00p3.

[19] Romans 3:23; Philippians 2:3.

[20] Bari Weiss, "Resignation Letter," July 14, 2020, https://www.bariweiss.com/resignation-letter.

[21] Ibid.

[22] Daniel Radosh, "The Good Book Business," The New Yorker December 11, 2006, https://www.newyorker.com/magazine/2006/12/18/the-good-book-business; "Best-Selling Book," Guinness World Records, https://www.guinnessworldrecords.com/world-records/best-selling-book-of-non-fiction.

[23] Quoted in Emma Colton, "Don Lemon Wonders 'How Can You Not Be Racist' If Raised in U.S.," Washington Examiner June 14, 2020, https://www.washingtonexaminer.com/news/don-lemon-wonders-how-can-you-not-be-racist-if-raised-in-us.

[24] @BetoORourke, August 18, 2019, https://twitter.com/BetoORourke/sta-

tus/1163107323373600769.

[25] Quoted in Yohuru Williams, "Why Thomas Jefferson's Anti-Slavery Passage Was Removed from the Declaration of Independence," History Channel June 29, 2020, https://www.history.com/news/declaration-of-independence-deleted-anti-slavery-clause-jefferson.

[26] Ryan Williams, "America Was Not Conceived in Racism," Newsweek July 15, 2020, https://www.newsweek.com/america-was-not-conceived-racism-opinion-1518091; Tom Lindsay, "'After All, Didn't America Invent Slavery,'" Forbes August 30, 2019, https://www.forbes.com/sites/tomlindsay/2019/08/30/after-all-didnt-america-invent-slavery/#494f6077ef6e; Act Prohibiting Importation of Slaves, P.L. 9-22.

[27] Quoted in Damon Root, "'A Glorious Liberty Document,'" Reason October 2006, https://reason.com/2006/10/01/a-glorious-liberty-document-2/.

[28] Max Fisher, "A Fascinating Map of the World's Most and Least Racially Tolerant Countries," The Washington Post May 15, 2013, https://www.washingtonpost.com/news/worldviews/wp/2013/05/15/a-fascinating-map-of-the-worlds-most-and-least-racially-tolerant-countries/.

[29] Jacob Poushter and Janell Fetterolf, "How People Around the World View Diversity in Their Countries," Pew Research Center, April 22, 2019, https://www.pewresearch.org/global/2019/04/22/how-people-around-the-world-view-diversity-in-their-countries/.

[30] United Nations, Department of Economic and Social Affairs, Population Division, "International Migrant Stock 2019," https://www.un.org/en/development/desa/population/migration/data/estimates2/data/UN_MigrantStockTotal_2019.xlsx, Table 1: International Migrant Stock at Mid-Year by Sex and by Major Area, Region, Country, or Area, 1990-2019; U.S. Citizenship and Immigration Services, "Naturalization Fact Sheet," June 25, 2019, https://www.uscis.gov/news/news-releases/naturalization-fact-sheet.

[31] Maria Krysan and Sarah Patton Moberg, "Trends in Racial Attitudes," University of Illinois Institute of Government and Public Affairs, August 25, 2016, https://igpa.uillinois.edu/programs/racial-attitudes.

[32] MSU Today, "The Truth Behind Racial Disparities in Fatal Police Shootings," July 22, 2019, https://msutoday.msu.edu/news/2019/the-truth-behind-racial-disparities-in-fatal-police-shootings/; David Johnson, et al., "Officer Characteristics and Racial Disparities in Fatal Officer-Involved Shootings," Proceedings of the National Academy of Sciences 116:32 (July 22, 2019), https://www.pnas.org/content/116/32/15877.

[33] Prager University, "America Was Founded on Freedom Not Slavery," November 20, 2019, https://www.prageru.com/video/america-was-founded-on-freedom-not-slavery/.

[34] Lindsay, "'After All, Didn't America Invent Slavery?'"

[35] The New York Times Magazine, "The 1619 Project at the Smithsonian," October 30, 2019, https://www.nytimes.com/2019/10/30/magazine/1619-project-live-at-the-smithsonian.html.

[36] Nikole Hannah-Jones, "America Wasn't a Democracy, Until Black Americans Made It One," The New York Times Magazine August 14, 2019, https://www.nytimes.com/interactive/2019/08/14/magazine/black-history-american-democracy.html.

[37] Andrew Sullivan, "The New York Times Has Abandoned Liberalism for Activism," New York September 13, 2019, https://nymag.com/intelligencer/2019/09/andrew-sullivan-ny-times-abandons-liberalism-for-activism.html.

[38] Jake Silverstein, "Why We Published the 1619 Project," The New York Times Magazine December 20, 2019, https://www.nytimes.com/interactive/2019/12/20/magazine/1619-intro.html.

[39] Hannah-Jones, "America Wasn't a Democracy."

[40] Jake Silverstein, "An Update to the 1619 Project," The New York Times Magazine March 11, 2020, https://www.nytimes.com/2020/03/11/magazine/an-update-to-the-1619-project.html.

[41] Quoted in "We Respond to Historians Who Critiqued the 1619 Project," The New York Times Magazine December 20, 2019, https://www.nytimes.com/2019/12/20/magazine/we-respond-to-the-historians-who-critiqued-the-1619-project.html.

[42] Hannah-Jones, "America Wasn't a Democracy."

[43] Ibid.

[44] Woodson Center, "'When Whites Were at Their Worst, Blacks Were at Their Best:' The 1619 Project Has The New York Times; 1776 Has the Facts" February 13, 2020, https://woodsoncenter.org/2020/02/13/whites-worst-blacks-best-1619-project-ny-times-1776-facts/; https://1776unites.com/.

[45] Amanda Sakuma, "Trump Did Better with Blacks, Hispanics, Than Romney in '12: Exit Polls," NBC News November 9, 2016, https://www.nbcnews.com/storyline/2016-election-day/trump-did-better-blacks-hispanics-romney-12-exit-polls-n681386.

[46] Quoted in Yoav Gonen and Carl Campanile, "Cuomo Says America 'Was Never That Great,'" New York Post August 15, 2018, https://nypost.com/2018/08/15/cuomo-says-america-was-never-that-great/.

[47] @BernieSanders, September 26, 2015, https://twitter.com/BernieSanders/status/647825918954733568.

[48] "Leonardo DiCaprio at the UN: 'Climate Change Is Not Hysteria – It's a Fact," The Guardian September 23, 2014, https://www.theguardian.com/environment/2014/sep/23/leonarodo-dicaprio-un-climate-change-speech-new-york.

[49] Jason West, "CO2 Makes Up Just 0.04% of Earth's Atmosphere. Here's Why Its Impact Is So Massive," The Conversation September 16, 2019, https://www.sciencealert.com/co2-is-only-a-tiny-part-of-our-atmosphere-but-it-has-a-huge-influence-here-s-why.

[50] Paul Knappenberger and Patrick Michaels, "0.02C Temperature Rise Averted: The Vital Number Missing from the EPA's 'By the Numbers' Fact Sheet," Cato at Liberty June 11, 2014, https://www.cato.org/blog/002degc-temperature-rise-averted-vital-number-missing-epas-numbers-fact-sheet.

[51] National Oceanic and Atmospheric Administration, Geophysical Fluid Dynamics Laboratory, "Global Warming and Hurricanes," June 12, 2020, https://www.gfdl.noaa.gov/global-warming-and-hurricanes/.

[52] International Energy Agency, "Global CO2 Emissions in 2019," February 11, 2020, https://www.iea.org/articles/global-co2-emissions-in-2019.

[53] Philip Shabecoff, "Global Warming Has Begun, Expert Tells Senate," The New York Times June 24, 1988, https://www.nytimes.com/1988/06/24/us/global-warming-has-begun-expert-tells-senate.html.

[54] Peter Spielmann, "U.N. Predicts Disaster if Global Warming Not Checked," Associated Press June 29, 1989, https://apnews.com/bd45c372caf118ec99964ea547880cd0.

[55] Robert Bradley, Jr., "Climate Alarm: Failed Prognostications," Institute for Energy Research, June 22, 2018, https://www.instituteforenergyresearch.org/climate-change/climate-alarm-failed-prognostications/.

[56] BBC News, "PM Warns of Climate 'Catastrophe,'" October 19, 2009, http://news.bbc.co.uk/2/hi/uk_news/8313672.stm.

[57] John Vidal, "Arctic Expert Predicts Final Collapse of Sea Ice Within Four Years," The Guardian September 17, 2012, https://www.theguardian.com/environment/2012/sep/17/arctic-collapse-sea-ice.

[58] David Whitehouse, "The Truth about the Global Warming Pause," The Spectator June 28, 2017, https://www.spectator.co.uk/article/the-truth-about-the-global-warming-pause.

[59] Stephen Moore, "Follow the (Climate Change) Money," The Washington Times December 16, 2018, https://www.washingtontimes.com/news/2018/dec/16/follow-the-climate-change-money/.

[60] Judith Curry, "Science, Uncertainty, and Debate," June 22, 2015, https://judithcurry.com/2015/06/22/science-uncertainty-and-advocacy/.

[61] Collister Johnson, "Eliminating Fossil Fuels Now Would Have No Effect on Temps," Climate Change Dispatch March 4, 2020, https://climatechangedispatch.com/eliminating-fossil-fuels-no-effect-temps/.

[62] "Emissions Slashed Today Won't Slow Warming Until Mid-Century," The Economist July 11, 2020, https://www.economist.com/science-and-technology/2020/07/11/emissions-slashed-today-wont-slow-warming-until-mid-century.

[63] "Green New Deal FAQ," February 7, 2019, https://apps.npr.org/documents/document.html?id=5729035-Green-New-Deal-FAQ.

[64] Ibid.

[65] Ibid.

[66] Robin DiAngelo, White Fragility: Why It's So Hard for White People to Talk about Racism (Boston: Beacon Press, 2018).

[67] Quoted in Hannah Sparks, "Oprah Labeled a 'Fraud' for Calling Out 'White Privilege' since She's So Rich," New York Post August 5, 2020, https://nypost.com/2020/08/05/oprah-criticized-for-calling-out-white-privilege-since-shes-rich/.

[68] Cited in American Foundation for Suicide Prevention, "Suicide Statistics," March 1, 2020, https://afsp.org/suicide-statistics/.

[69] Cited in Vincent Harinam and Rob Henderson, "Why White Privilege Is Wrong – Part I," Quillette August 22, 2019, https://quillette.com/2019/08/22/why-white-privilege-is-wrong-part-1/.

[70] Raj Chetty, et al., "Where Is the Land of Opportunity: The Geography of Intergenerational Mobility in the United States," Quarterly Journal of Economics 129:4 (June 2014), https://scholar.

harvard.edu/files/hendren/files/mobility_geo.pdf; Isabel Sawhill and Joanna Venator, "Three Policies to Close the Class Divide in Family Formation," Brookings Institution, January 21, 2014, https://www.brookings.edu/blog/social-mobility-memos/2014/01/21/three-policies-to-close-the-class-divide-in-family-formation/.

[71] Cited in Dennis Prager, "The Fallacy of 'White Privilege,'" National Review February 16, 2016, https://www.nationalreview.com/2016/02/white-privilege-myth-reality/.

[72] Bureau of Labor Statistics, "Asian Women and Men Earned More than Their White, Black, and Hispanic Counterparts in 2017," TED: The Economics Daily August 29, 2018, https://www.bls.gov/opub/ted/2018/asian-women-and-men-earned-more-than-their-white-black-and-hispanic-counterparts-in-2017.htm.

[73] Census Bureau, "Educational Attainment in the United States: 2019," March 30, 2020, https://www2.census.gov/programs-surveys/demo/tables/educational-attainment/2019/cps-detailed-tables/table-3.xlsx, Table 3: Detailed Years of School Completed by People 25 Years and Over by Sex, Age Groups, Race, and Hispanic Origin.

[74] Cited in Harinam and Henderson, "Why White Privilege Is Wrong."

[75] Ibid.

[76] Jon Greenberg, "10 Examples That Prove White Privilege Exists in Every Aspect Imaginable," Yes!, July 24, 2017, https://www.yesmagazine.org/social-justice/2017/07/24/10-examples-that-prove-white-privilege-exists-in-every-aspect-imaginable/.

[77] Stephanie Ebbert, "Directories Listed Warren as Minority," Boston Globe April 30, 2012, http://archive.boston.com/news/local/massachusetts/articles/2012/04/30/elizabeth_warren_was_listed_as_a_minority_professor_in_law_directories_in_the_80s_and_90s/.

[78] Asma Khalid, "Warren Releases DNA Results, Challenges Trump over Native American Ancestry," NPR October 15, 2018, https://www.npr.org/2018/10/15/657468655/warren-releases-dna-results-challenges-trump-over-native-american-ancestry.

[79] Prager, "The Fallacy of 'White Privilege.'"

[80] John McWhorter, "The Dehumanizing Condescension of White Fragility," The Atlantic July 15, 2020, https://www.theatlantic.com/ideas/archive/2020/07/dehumanizing-condescension-white-fragility/614146/.

[81] @JoeBiden, July 27, 2020, https://twitter.com/JoeBiden/status/1287788085888065540.

[82] Hillary Rodham Clinton, What Happened (New York: Simon and Schuster, 2017).

[83] Benjamin Frost, Peggy Hazard, and Desi Kimmins, "The Real Gap: Fixing the Gender Pay Divide," Korn Ferry Hay Group, February 2015, https://focus.kornferry.com/wp-content/uploads/2015/02/KFHG_Gender_Pay_Gap_whitepaper.pdf; PayScale, "The State of the Gender Pay Gap 2020," March 31, 2020, https://www.payscale.com/data/gender-pay-gap.

[84] Valentin Bolotnyy and Natalia Emanuel, "Why Do Women Earn Less Than Men? Evidence from Bus and Train Operators," Working Paper, November 28, 2018, https://scholar.harvard.edu/files/bolotnyy/files/be_gendergap.pdf.

[85] American Express, "The State of Women-Owned Businesses, 2019," September 23, 2019, https://s1.q4cdn.com/692158879/files/doc_library/file/2019-state-of-women-owned-businesses-report.pdf, p. 3; SCORE, "The Megaphone of Main Street: Women's Entrepreneurship," April 2018, https://s3.amazonaws.com/mentoring.redesign/s3fs-public/SCORE-Megaphone-of-Main-Street-Women%E2%80%99s-Entrepreneurship-Spring-2018_1.pdf, p. 7.

[86] Census Bureau, Educational Attainment in the United States: 2019, https://www2.census.gov/programs-surveys/demo/tables/educational-attainment/time-series/cps-historical-time-series/taba-1.xlsx, Table A-1: Years of School Completed by People 25 Years and over, by Age and Sex: Selected Years 1940 to 2019.

[87] National Center for Education Statistics, Digest of Education Statistics, https://nces.ed.gov/programs/digest/current_tables.asp, Table 301.10: Enrollment, Staff, and Degrees/Certificates Conferred in Degree-Granting and Non-Degree-Granting Postsecondary Institutions, by Control and Level of Institution, Sex of Student, Type of Staff, and Level of Degree: Fall 2017 and 2016-17, and Table 301.20: Historical Summary of Faculty, Enrollment, Degrees Conferred, and Finances in Degree-Granting Postsecondary Institutions: Selected Years, 1869-70 through 2016-17.

[88] American Association of Medical Colleges, "2019 Facts: Applicants and Matriculants Data," December 2019, https://www.aamc.org/data-reports/students-residents/interactive-data/2019-facts-applicants-and-matriculants-data, Table A-7.2: Applicants, First-Time Applicants, Acceptees, and Matriculants to U.S. Medical Schools by Sex, 2010-2011 through 2019-2020, and Chart 3: Matriculants to U.S. Medical Schools by Sex, 1980-1981 through

2019-2020.

[89] Guido Cortes, Nir Jaimovich, and Henry Siu, "The 'End of Men" and Rise of Women in the High-Skilled Labor Market," National Bureau of Economic Research Working Paper 24274, November 2018, https://www.nber.org/papers/w24274.pdf.

[90] Boadie Dunlop and Tanja Mletzko, "Will Current Socioeconomic Trends Produce a Depressing Future for Men?" British Journal of Psychiatry 198:3 (March 2011), https://www.ncbi.nlm.nih.gov/pmc/articles/PMC3046178/.

[91] Census Bureau, "School Enrollment in the United States: October 2018 – Detailed Tables," December 3, 2019, https://www2.census.gov/programs-surveys/demo/tables/school-enrollment/2018/2018-cps/tab01-01.xlsx, Table 1: Enrollment Status of the Population Three Years Old and Over, by Sex, Age, Race, Hispanic Origin, Foreign Born, and Foreign-Born Parentage: October 2018.

[92] Andrew Sum, et al., "The Consequences of Dropping Out of High School: Joblessness and Jailing for High School Dropouts and the High Cost for Taxpayers," Center for Labor Market Studies, October 2009, https://www.prisonpolicy.org/scans/The_Consequences_of_Dropping_Out_of_High_School.pdf, Chart 7: Percent of 16-24 Year Old Males in the U.S. Who Were Institutionalized in 2006-2007 by Selected School Enrollment/Educational Attainment Group, p. 10.

[93] Melissa Kearney, et al., "Ten Facts about Crime and Incarceration in the United States," Brookings Institution Hamilton Project, May 2014, https://www.brookings.edu/wp-content/uploads/2016/06/v8_THP_10CrimeFacts.pdf, p. 11.

[94] Quoted in Michael Burke, "Ocasio-Cortez: Capitalism Is 'Irredeemable,'" The Hill March 10, 2019, https://thehill.com/homenews/house/433394-ocasio-cortez-capitalism-is-irredeemable.

[95] @MarkRuffalo, December 1, 2019, https://twitter.com/MarkRuffalo/status/1201176660252475392.

[96] Maxim Pinkovskiy and Xavier Sala-i-Martin, "Parametric Estimations of the World Distribution of Income," National Bureau of Economic Research Working Paper 15433, October 2009, https://www.nber.org/papers/w15433.pdf.

[97] Ibid., Table 5: Regional Poverty Rates, $1/day, p. 69.

[98] Census Bureau, "Extended Measures of Well-Being: Living Conditions in the United States, 2011," September 2013, https://web.archive.org/web/20131119142230/http:/www.census.gov/hhes/well-being/publications/extended-11.html, Table 1: Percent of Households Reporting Consumer Durables, For Householders 15 Years and Older, by Selected Characteristics, 2011, and Table 2: Percent of Households Reporting Favorable Housing Conditions by Selected Characteristics, For Householders 15 Years and Older, 2011.

[99] James Agresti, "The Poorest 20% of Americans Are Richer on Average Than Most Nations of Europe," Just Facts August 26, 2019, https://www.justfacts.com/news_poorest_americans_richer_than_europe.asp.

[100] World Bank, "Principles and Practice in Measuring Global Poverty," January 13, 2016, https://www.worldbank.org/en/news/feature/2016/01/13/principles-and-practice-in-measuring-global-poverty.

[101] Hannah Hartig, "Stark Partisan Divisions in Americans' Views of 'Socialism,' 'Capitalism,'" Pew Research Center, June 25, 2019, https://www.pewresearch.org/fact-tank/2019/06/25/stark-partisan-divisions-in-americans-views-of-socialism-capitalism/.

[102] Ibid.; Emily Ekins, "What Americans Think About Poverty, Wealth, and Work: Findings from the Cato Institute 2019 Welfare, Work, and Wealth National Survey," Cato Institute, September 24, 2019, https://www.cato.org/sites/cato.org/files/2019-09/Cato2019WelfareWorkWealthSurveyReport%20%281%29.pdf, p. 29.

[103] Philanthropy Roundtable, "Who Gives Most to Charity?" https://www.philanthropyroundtable.org/almanac/statistics/who-gives.

[104] Amy Clark, "Castro: I Am Not Rich," CBS News May 16, 2006, https://www.cbsnews.com/news/castro-i-am-not-rich/.

[105] Liam Doyle, "Kim Jong-Un Net Worth: What Is the North Korean Supreme Leader Worth," Express May 3, 2020, https://www.express.co.uk/news/world/1277270/Kim-Jong-Un-net-worth-what-is-Kim-Jong-un-net-worth-North-Korea.

[106] Fox News, "Hugo Chavez Daughter is the Richest Individual in Venezuela, Report Claims," August 10, 2015, https://www.foxnews.com/world/hugo-chavez-daughter-is-the-richest-individual-in-venezuela-report-claims.

[107] Rob Wile, "Is Vladimir Putin Secretly the Richest Man in the World?" Money January 23, 2017, https://money.com/vladimir-putin-net-worth/; Cristina Maza, "Is Vladimir Putin the World's Richest

Person? Congress Sets Out to Find Russian President's Hidden Net Worth," Newsweek March 4, 2019, https://www.newsweek.com/vladimir-putin-richest-person-world-net-worth-1351011.

[108] Census Bureau, "Five-Year Trends Available for Median Household Income, Poverty Rates, and Computer and Internet Use, December 6, 2018, https://www.census.gov/newsroom/press-releases/2018/2013-2017-acs-5year.html; Paul Bedard, "Swamp's Gold: Six of Ten Richest Counties in America Are D.C. Suburbs, 10 of the Top 20," Washington Examiner December 20, 2018, https://www.washingtonexaminer.com/washington-secrets/swamps-gold-6-of-10-richest-counties-in-america-are-dc-suburbs-10-of-the-top-20.

[109] James Carville, Had Enough? A Handbook for Fighting Back (New York: Simon and Schuster, 2003), p. 21.

[110] Lyndon Johnson, State of the Union Address before a Joint Session of Congress, January 8, 1964, https://www.americanrhetoric.com/speeches/lbj1964stateoftheunion.htm.

[111] Robert Rector and Rachel Sheffield, "The War on Poverty after 50 Years," Heritage Foundation Backgrounder No. 2955, September 15, 2014, http://thf_media.s3.amazonaws.com/2014/pdf/BG2955.pdf.

[112] Howard Husock, "Public Housing and Rental Subsidies," Cato Institute, February 23, 2017, https://www.downsizinggovernment.org/hud/public-housing-rental-subsidies.

[113] Christine Kim and Robert Rector, "Welfare Reform Turns Ten: Evidence Shows Reduced Dependence, Poverty," Heritage Foundation WebMemo No. 1183, August 1, 2006, https://www.heritage.org/welfare/report/welfare-reform-turns-ten-evidence-shows-reduced-dependence-poverty.

[114] Lindsey Burke and David Muhlhausen, "Head Start Impact Evaluation Report Finally Released," Heritage Foundation Issue Brief No. 3823, January 10, 2013, http://thf_media.s3.amazonaws.com/2013/pdf/ib3823.pdf.

[115] Raj Chetty, et al., "The Fading American Dream: Trends in Absolute Income Mobility since 1940," National Bureau of Economic Research Working Paper 22910, December 2016, https://www.nber.org/papers/w22910.pdf.

[116] National Center for Education Statistics, "The Nation's Report Card 2015: Mathematics and Reading at Grade 12," https://www.nationsreportcard.gov/reading_math_g12_2015/.

[117] Ibid.

[118] Ibid.

[119] NCES, Digest of Education Statistics, Table 221.85: Average National Assessment of Educational Progress (NAEP) Reading Scale Score, by Age and Selected Student Characteristics: Selected Years, 1971 through 2012.

[120] National Center for Education Statistics, "The Nation's Report Card: Achievement Gaps Dashboard," https://www.nationsreportcard.gov/dashboards/achievement_gaps.aspx.

[121] Ibid.

[122] NCES, Digest of Education Statistics, Table 236.10: Summary of Expenditures for Public Elementary and Secondary Education and Other Related Programs, by Purpose: Selected Years, 1919-20 through 2016-17, and Table 236.15: Current Expenditures and Current Expenditures Per Pupil in Public Elementary and Secondary Schools: 1989-90 through 2029-30.

[123] Ibid., Table 236.15. Calculation based on $13,480 spending per pupil in 2019-20 based on average daily attendance (in constant dollars), and $9,516 spending per pupil in 1989-90 based on average daily attendance (in constant dollars).

[124] Ibid., Table 201.10: Historical Summary of Public Elementary and Secondary School Statistics: Selected Years, 1869-70 through 2016-17.

[125] Ibid., Table 213.10: Staff Employed in Public Elementary and Secondary Education School Systems, by Type of Assignment: Selected Years, 1949-50 through Fall 2017.

[126] Ibid.

[127] Ibid.

[128] Ibid., Table 208.10: Public Elementary and Secondary Pupil/Teacher Ratios, by Selected School Characteristics: Selected Years, Fall 1990 through Fall 2016.

[129] Jeff Allen, "Trends in ACT Composite Scores among Homeschooled Students," ACT Data Byte 2015-2, May 18, 2015, https://www.act.org/content/dam/act/unsecured/documents/Info-Brief-2015-2.pdf.

[130] Census Bureau, "Historical Poverty Tables: People and Families – 1959 to 2018," https://www2.census.gov/programs-surveys/cps/tables/time-series/historical-poverty-people/hstpov2.xls, Table 2: Poverty Status of People by Family Relationship, Race, and Hispanic Origin.

[131] Gene Steuerle, Testimony before the House Ways and Means Subcommittees on Human Resources and Select Revenue Measures on "Marginal Tax Rates, Work, and the Nation's Real Tax System," June 27, 2012, https://www.taxpolicycenter.org/sites/default/files/alfresco/publication-pdfs/901508-Marginal-Tax-Rates-Work-and-the-Nation-s-Real-Tax-System.PDF.

[132] Congressional Budget Office, "The Budget and Economic Outlook: 2014 to 2024," February 4, 2014, https://www.cbo.gov/sites/default/files/113th-congress-2013-2014/reports/45010-outlook-2014feb0.pdf, Appendix C: Labor Market Effects of the Affordable Care Act: Updated Estimates," pp. 117-27.

[133] David Altig, et al., "Marginal Net Taxation of Americans' Labor Supply," National Bureau of Economic Research Working Paper 27164, May 2020, https://www.nber.org/papers/w27164.pdf.

[134] Congressional Budget Office, "Medicaid – CBO's Baseline as of March 6, 2020," https://www.cbo.gov/system/files/2020-03/51301-2020-03-medicaid.pdf; NCES, Digest of Education Statistics, Table 235.10: Revenues for Public Elementary and Secondary Schools, by Source of Funds: Selected Years, 1919-20 through 2016-17.

[135] Katherine Baicker, et al., "The Oregon Experiment: Effects of Medicaid on Clinical Outcomes," New England Journal of Medicine May 2, 2013, https://www.nejm.org/doi/full/10.1056/NEJMsa1212321.

[136] See for instance Government Accountability Office, "VA Health Care: Reliability of Reported Outpatient Medical Appointment Wait Times and Scheduling Oversight Need Improvement," Report GAO-13-130, January 18, 2013, https://www.gao.gov/assets/660/651076.pdf, and The American Legion, "Epidemic of VA Mismanagement," https://www.legion.org/documents/legion/pdf/va_epidemic.pdf.

[137] Department of Housing and Urban Development, "2019 Point-in-Time Estimates of Homelessness in the U.S.," https://www.hud.gov/2019-point-in-time-estimates-of-homelessness-in-US.

[138] The Young Turks, "Elizabeth Warren Interview on TYT," February 20, 2019, https://www.youtube.com/watch?v=8yyMvFBTIXU.

[139] @Kamala Harris, April 21, 2017, https://twitter.com/KamalaHarris/status/855566507526565888; Michelle Ye Hee Lee, "Sen. Kamala Harris' Claim that an 'Undocumented Immigrant Is Not a Criminal," The Washington Post April 26, 2017, https://www.washingtonpost.com/news/fact-checker/wp/2017/04/26/sen-kamala-harriss-claim-that-an-undocumented-immigrant-is-not-a-criminal/.

[140] Quoted in Andras Gergely, "Orban Accuses Soros of Stoking Refugee Wave to Weaken Europe," Bloomberg October 30, 2015, https://www.bloomberg.com/news/articles/2015-10-30/orban-accuses-soros-of-stoking-refugee-wave-to-weaken-europe.

[141] George Borjas, "Yes, Immigration Hurts American Workers," Politico September 12, 2016, https://www.politico.com/magazine/story/2016/09/trump-clinton-immigration-economy-unemployment-jobs-214216.

[142] Neil Esipova, Anita Pugliese, and Julie Ray, "More than 750 Million Worldwide Would Migrate if They Could," Gallup, December 10, 2018, https://news.gallup.com/poll/245255/750-million-worldwide-migrate.aspx.

[143] Federal Bureau of Prisons, "Inmate Citizenship," August 22, 2020, https://www.bop.gov/about/statistics/statistics_inmate_citizenship.jsp; Government Accountability Office, "Criminal Alien Statistics: Information on Incarcerations, Arrests, Convictions, Costs, and Removals," Report GAO-18-433, July 17, 2018, https://www.gao.gov/assets/700/693162.pdf, p. 18; Michelangelo Landgrave and Alex Nowrasteh, "Illegal Immigrant Incarceration Rates, 2010-2018: Demographics and Policy Implications," Cato Institute Policy Analysis No. 890, April 21, 2020, https://www.cato.org/publications/policy-analysis/illegal-immigrant-incarceration-rates-2010-2018-demographics-policy.

[144] Matt O'Brien and Spencer Raley, "The Fiscal Burden of Illegal Immigration on United States Taxpayers," Federation for Immigration Reform, September 27, 2017, https://www.fairus.org/sites/default/files/2017-09/Fiscal-Burden-of-Illegal-Immigration-2017.pdf.

[145] Immigration and Customs Enforcement, "Combating Gangs," February 13, 2020, https://www.ice.gov/features/gangs.

[146] Medecins sans Frontieres, "Forced to Flee Central America's Northern Triangle: A Neglected Humanitarian Crisis," May 2017, https://www.doctorswithoutborders.org/sites/default/files/2018-06/msf_forced-to-flee-central-americas-northern-triangle.pdf, p. 12.

[147] Centers for Disease Control, "Heroin Overdose Data," March 19, 2020, https://www.cdc.gov/drugoverdose/data/heroin.html.

[148] Department of Homeland Security, 2018 Yearbook of Immigration Statistics, October 2019,

https://www.dhs.gov/sites/default/files/publications/immigration-statistics/yearbook/2018/yearbook_immigration_statistics_2018.pdf, Table 1: Persons Obtaining Lawful Permanent Resident Status: Fiscal Years 1820 to 2018, p. 5.

[149] Organization for Economic Cooperation and Development, International Migration Outlook 2019, October 15, 2019, https://www.oecd-ilibrary.org/docserver/c3e35eec-en.pdf, Table 1.1: Inflows of Permanent Immigrants into OECD Countries, 2010-17, p. 21.

[150] Immigration and Nationality Act of 1965, P.L. 89-236.

[151] Steven Camarota and Karen Zeigler, "The Impact of Legal and Illegal Immigration on the Apportionment of Seats in the U.S. House of Representatives in 2020," Center for Immigration Studies, December 19, 2019, https://cis.org/sites/default/files/2019-12/camarota-apportionment-12-19_1.pdf.

[152] Quoted in Eric Bradner, Sarah Mucha, and Arlette Saenz, "Biden: 'If You Have a Problem Figuring Out Whether You're for Me or Trump, Then You Ain't Black,'" CNN May 22, 2020, https://www.cnn.com/2020/05/22/politics/biden-charlamagne-tha-god-you-aint-black/index.html.

[153] MSNBC, "Trump Tries to Portray Biden as a Racist," Morning Joe August 7, 2020, https://www.youtube.com/watch?v=8ZJOean2-kE.

[154] Dahleen Glanton, "White America, If You Want to Know Who's Responsible for Racism, Look in the Mirror," Chicago Tribune May 31, 2020, https://www.chicagotribune.com/columns/dahleen-glanton/ct-racism-white-people-george-floyd-20200531-tmdbj52ownc7fegdargh75k4qq-story.html.

[155] Census Bureau, "Historical Poverty Tables: People and Families – 1959 to 2018," April 6, 2020, https://www2.census.gov/programs-surveys/cps/tables/time-series/historical-poverty-people/hstpov4.xls, Table 4: Poverty Status of Families, by Type of Family, Presence of Related Children, Race, and Hispanic Origin.

[156] Section 13823 of the Tax Cuts and Jobs Act, P.L. 115-97; Naomi Jagoda, "Tlaib Introduces Bill to Repeal 'Opportunity Zones,'" The Hill November 22, 2019, https://thehill.com/policy/finance/471709-tlaib-offers-bill-to-repeal-opportunity-zones; Nihal Krishan, "AOC Introduces Amendment to Defund Trump 'Opportunity Zones,'" Washington Examiner July 23, 2020, https://www.washingtonexaminer.com/news/aoc-introduces-amendment-to-defund-trump-opportunity-zones.

[157] Serving Our Children, "Program Fact Sheet: D.C. Opportunity Scholarship Program, 2019-20," January 2020, https://servingourchildrendc.org/wp-content/uploads/2020/01/DC-OSP-Program-Fact-Sheet-SY-2019-20-1.pdf; Biden for President, "Biden-Sanders Unity Task Force Recommendations," July 8, 2020, https://assets.documentcloud.org/documents/6983111/UNITY-TASK-FORCE-RECOMMENDATIONS.pdf, p. 83.

[158] Tara Jatlaoui, et al., "Abortion Surveillance – United States, 2016," Centers for Disease Control Morbidity and Mortality Weekly Report 68:11 (November 29, 2019), https://www.cdc.gov/mmwr/volumes/68/ss/ss6811a1.htm; Census Bureau, "Quick Facts," https://www.census.gov/quickfacts/fact/table/US/LFE046218.

[159] Judith Katz, "Some Aspects and Assumptions of White Culture in the United States," Kaleel Jamison Consulting Group, 1990, http://www.cascadia.edu/discover/about/diversity/documents/Some%20Aspects%20and%20Assumptions%20of%20White%20Culture%20in%20the%20United%20States.pdf.

[160] National Museum of African American History and Culture, "Whiteness," July 17, 2020, https://nmaahc.si.edu/learn/talking-about-race/topics/whiteness.

[161] Benenson Strategy Group, "Key Takeaways: National Education Polling Results," October 7, 2019, http://dfer.org/wp-content/uploads/2019/10/Interested-Parties-Memo-October-2019.pdf.

[162] New York University, The Margaret Sanger Papers Project, "Birth Control or Race Control? Sanger and the Negro Project," Newsletter #28 (Fall 2001), https://www.nyu.edu/projects/sanger/articles/bc_or_race_control.php; Margaret Sanger, "High Lights in the History of Birth Control," October 1923, https://www.nyu.edu/projects/sanger/webedition/app/documents/show.php?sanger-Doc=306641.xml&_ga=2.160207933.1236211671.1597956800-2145738491.1572883971.

[163] New York City Department of Health and Mental Hygiene, "Summary of Vital Statistics 2017: The City of New York," July 2019, https://www1.nyc.gov/assets/doh/downloads/pdf/vs/2017sum.pdf, Table IM4: Live Births and Infant Mortality, Overall and by Mother's Racial/Ethnic Group, New York City, 2013-2017, p. 80, and Table PO19: Induced Terminations of Pregnancy by Woman's Martial Status, Age, and Ethnic Group, New York City, 2013-2017, p. 97.

[164] Rector and Sheffield, "The War on Poverty after 50 Years."

[165] Bureau of Labor Statistics, "The Employment Situation – October 2019," November 1, 2019,

https://www.bls.gov/news.release/archives/empsit_11012019.pdf, Summary Table A: Household Data, Seasonally Adjusted, p. 4.

[166] First Step Act, P.L. 115-391.

[167] @Politico, August 27, 2020, https://twitter.com/politico/status/1299165900130734087.

[168] Quoted in Caleb Parke, "Alice Marie Johnson Responds to Politico's Tweet She Was 'Propped Up' by Trump 2020: 'I'm not a Puppet,'" Fox News August 28, 2020, https://www.foxnews.com/politics/rnc-alice-marie-johnson-trump-criminal-justice.

[169] Black Lives Matter, "What We Believe," https://blacklivesmatter.com/what-we-believe/.

Southern Poverty Law Center, "Anti-LGBTQ," https://www.splcenter.org/fighting-hate/extremist-files/ideology/anti-lgbtq.

[171] Roger Kimball, "Racism, Inc.," American Greatness June 6, 2020, https://amgreatness.com/2020/06/06/racism-inc/.

[172] Dred Scott v. Sandford, 60 U.S. 393 (1857).

[173] Ciara O'Rourke, "No, The Democratic Party Didn't Create the Ku Klux Klan," Politifact October 24, 2018, https://www.politifact.com/factchecks/2018/oct/24/blog-posting/no-democratic-party-didnt-create-klu-klux-klan/.

[174] Plessy v. Ferguson, 163 U.S. 537 (1896).

[175] Civil Rights Act of 1957, P.L. 85-315; House Roll Call Vote 42 of 1957 (85th Congress, 1st Session), June 18, 1957, https://www.govtrack.us/congress/votes/85-1957/h42; Senate Roll Call Vote 75 of 1957 (85th Congress, 1st Session), August 7, 1957, https://www.govtrack.us/congress/votes/85-1957/s75.

[176] Civil Rights Act of 1964, P.L. 88-352; Senate Roll Call Vote 409 of 1964, June 19, 1964 (88th Congress, 2nd Session), https://www.govtrack.us/congress/votes/88-1964/s409; House Roll Call Vote 182 of 1964, July 2, 1964 (88th Congress, 2nd Session), https://www.govtrack.us/congress/votes/88-1964/h182.

[177] Rector and Sheffield, "The War on Poverty after 50 Years," pp. 8-10.

[178] @MstthewDowd, September 2, 2019, https://twitter.com/matthewjdowd/status/1168699946939363328.

[179] Adam Litpak, "'We the People' Loses Its Appeal with People Around the World," The New York Times February 7, 2012, https://www.nytimes.com/2012/02/07/us/we-the-people-loses-appeal-with-people-around-the-world.html.

[180] Quoted in Ibid.

[181] John Greenwald, "A Gift to All Nations," Time July 6, 1987, http://content.time.com/time/magazine/article/0,9171,964901,00.html.

[182] Timothy Snowball, "The Founding Fathers of Our Limited Government: James Madison and the Fight for the Separation of Powers," Pacific Legal Foundation, June 10, 2019, https://pacificlegal.org/the-founding-fathers-of-our-limited-government-james-madison-and-the-fight-for-the-separation-of-powers/.

[183] Carrie Dann, "Republicans, Democrats Take Opposite Views on Nixing the Electoral College," NBC News May 6, 2019, https://www.nbcnews.com/politics/meet-the-press/republicans-democrats-take-opposite-views-nixing-electoral-college-n1001811.

[184] National Archives, "America's Founding Fathers: Delegates to the Constitutional Convention," https://web.archive.org/web/20161006143659/http://www.archives.gov/exhibits/charters/constitution_founding_fathers_overview.html.

[185] "Data: Most States Require History, But Not Civics," Education Week October 23, 2018, https://www.edweek.org/ew/section/multimedia/data-most-states-require-history-but-not.html.

[186] Sarah Hauer, "Paul Ryan Claims the U.S. Is the 'Oldest Democracy' in the World. Is He Right?" Politifact July 11, 2016, https://www.politifact.com/factchecks/2016/jul/11/paul-ryan/paul-ryan-claims-us-oldest-democracy-world-he-righ/.

[187] Eric Kaufmann, "The Great Awokening and the Second American Revolution," Quillette June 22, 2020, https://quillette.com/2020/06/22/toward-a-new-cultural-nationalism/.

[188] Jon Levine, "Andrew Sullivan Leaves New York Magazine, Blasts Colleagues Upon Exit," New York Post July 18, 2020, https://nypost.com/2020/07/18/andrew-sullivan-leaves-new-york-magazine-blasts-colleagues/.